SON OF DAVID
The Hidden Joseph

José Rodrigues

Copyright © 2009 by José Rodrigues

All rights Reserved

No part of this book may be reproduced, stored in a retrieval system, or transmitted by any means, electronic, mechanical, photocopying, recording, or otherwise, without written permission from the author or publisher. There is one exception. Brief passages may be quoted in articles or reviews.

Library and Archives Canada Cataloguing in Publication

CIP data on file with the National Library and Archives

ISBN 978-1-926582-17-7

Dedicated to my grandmothers,
Francoise Martin and Maria Virginia Rodrigues.

Special thanks to Father Paul Tinguely
who gave me the support that was instrumental
in the beginning and completing of this work.

"The life of Saint Joseph, lived in obedience to God's word, is an eloquent sign for all the disciples of Jesus who seek the unity of the Church. His example helps us to understand that it is only by complete submission to the will of God that we become effective workers in the service of his plan to gather together all mankind into one family, one assembly, one 'ecclesia.'"

Pope Benedict XVI
Yaoundé, Cameroon,
March 18, 2009

Foreword

While I was a seminarian in Ottawa, a visiting priest from Australia asked one March 19, the feast day of St. Joseph "What is there to celebrate about St. Joseph today? He didn't do much, and by the way, what can we say about him since there is not much written about him?" Having been taught at my elementary schools in Winnipeg by nuns of the Order of the Sisters of St. Joseph, I remember that on every feast day of St. Joseph we would have the day off so the Sisters could celebrate. I always felt that this saint did something good for me. So I disagreed with the Australian priest.

I reminded him that "St. Joseph must be important because, after all, he is the Protector of the Universal Church, and that's quite a job! No slouch there, for sure!" And of course, I said to him, "St. Joseph is the also the Protector of the Family and Patron Saint of Canada, and for that I'm very –happy— especially on this very important Feast day of the Church." I don't know if I was able to convince the priest and change his mind, but I tried.

José Rodrigues has good depth and understanding of St. Joseph. He explores the various avenues open to us and gives us a vast array of insights most often missed about St. Joseph. Our saint is revealed to us in both spiritual and insightful ways. Let yourself be guided by the author, José, to see St. Joseph in a different light. Let us learn that one can no longer see or speak of the foster-father of Jesus as a mere man, but rather, as a real, authentic, and holy man, ever faithful to the Will of God. May we seek this example of faith in each one of our lives, and also, to really begin to learn to ask for the intercession of St. Joseph, our loving Protector, for our needs.

- Father Paul Tinguely

Introduction

For as long as I can remember, I have had a special interest in St. Joseph of Nazareth. I can't exactly pinpoint when this first began, but while growing up I thought about this man. Some people just have special connections to certain people, be it their mother, father, a teacher, a fictional character, or sometimes even a saint. Why do we feel these special connections? What drives us to take refuge in the arms of these people?

Growing up, I didn't have much spiritual direction except for catechism classes at which I learned nothing I didn't already know. I do, however, owe gratitude to both my grandmothers as they planted that spiritual seed when I was still a young child. My mom's mother taught me to pray every night before bed. She taught me the Our Father and the Sign of the Cross. I remember only saying the Sign of the Cross when I was too sleepy to say the Our Father, but nonetheless it went straight to God. My father's mother, whom I call "Vo," taught me about the apparitions of Our Lady of Fatima, which took place in 1917, and about the miracles attributed to "*Nossa Senhora*." This would foster the beginning of my interest in who God was.

My parents didn't go to church, but when I spent time with my grandparents, I was able to ask questions and receive a few insights into this mystery of faith. I remember leaving Winnipeg every summer to visit my grandparents in the Manitoba countryside, in Ste. Amelie, where I would stay for two weeks. My grandparents had this big, hardcover children's Bible that I used to look at all the time. It was full of cool pictures of soldiers, kings, and prophets, and there was one image in particular to which I would pay extra attention: The Epiphany. In this picture, the Virgin Mary looks so beautiful and serene as she looks down at baby Jesus; her blue mantle is simple but radiant. The holy child is displayed, humble but adorable, as the newborn Saviour for mankind. The three wise men are magnificently robed and adorned as they pay homage to the infant King. It is one of the most recognisable scenes in the world, but someone is missing. Where is the man who received the newborn boy as his young wife delivered Him into our mortal world? Where is the man who would raise and nurture this child into manhood? Where is Joseph of Nazareth? He was hidden from me.

It turned out that Joseph was in fact present in this scene, but he was split in two. He was where the pages divide and since this was a thick book, the rise of pages on each side made it almost impossible to see this man unless you pressed hard on both sides to try to flatten the picture. He seemed to be more a spectator than a participant. Perhaps this is when my curiosity about him first began to take root, and I began to want to know who he was. Why was he hidden from me all this time?

Time passed, and I ended up visiting Portugal with my Vo. We went to the shrine of Fatima, where Our Lady appeared, and she bought me some children's books on the events that took place there during World War I. By now I was already familiar with the basics of this story, but there was something I had yet to discover. In addition to three shepherd children beholding the Blessed Virgin Mary atop a small Holm Oak tree, and in addition to the great Secrets and the Miracle of the Sun, something else happened. While the Miracle of the Sun was taking place (witnessed by over 70,000 people), the children were witnessing something else: they saw my hidden saint! The seers beheld St. Joseph in the sky, with the child Jesus in his arms, as they both traced the sign of the cross three times, blessing the assembled crowd. Joseph was still in the picture after all these years. I was so happy to read that he had not become obsolete as soon as Jesus was born! Though he didn't say anything, his actions spoke louder than words, just like in the Bible, which records not a single word spoken by Joseph. Rather it tells of his actions and conformity to God's Will, but no words.

In this little book I would like to discuss the Joseph I've come to know: a humble yet valiant man who, though he lived a modest life, is now great and powerful before the Throne of God. With this book I hope to present to you my hidden Joseph in a simple but comprehensive way. I've included many quotes from Scripture, tradition, and the saints, to help enrich the reader's understanding. I'm not a professional writer, nor am I a theologian, but I hope you'll accept this work of mine as something genuine and heartfelt.

Now, without spectacle or distraction, I pass this on to you, the reader, in the hope that you will have a better understanding of who this Hidden Joseph really is.

March 25, 2009
Feast of the Annunciation

The Just Man
Chapter 1: Son of David

> "For my thoughts are not your thoughts,
> nor are your ways my ways," says the Lord.
> "As high as the heavens are above the earth,
> so high are my ways above your ways,
> and my thoughts above your thoughts.
> **Isaiah 55:8-9**

There is a great difference between the judgments of man and those of God. For one thing, if we were divine and wanted to enter the mortal world and could pre-select the families we were born into, most of us would choose wealthy, noble parents so as to ensure a comfortable and privileged life. God Himself made this decision, but His choice was not the one most of us would make. Unlike us, God is not obsessed with the material world we live in. He is not distracted by expensive, shiny things. God Himself is all powerful yet all humility. God chose to enter this world not by being born in a great palace by the sea or in a majestic garden on a bed of lilies, but in a dank cave that housed beasts of burden, with a stone feedbox for a crib. His mother was not a queen or a noblewoman, but a simple Jewish girl named Mary. His father on earth was not an emperor or a valiant warrior, but merely a worker named Joseph. Joseph *did,* however, have royal blood and *could* lay claim to the throne. At the time of Jesus' birth, the foreign king Herod of Ascalon had usurped the throne of the sons of King David. Nevertheless, Joseph remained the rightful heir of the kings of Judea. He was of royal lineage and the Bible traces his genealogy in the Gospel of St. Matthew:

> ... Abraham begot Isaac, Isaac begot Jacob...
> Jesse begot David the king. And David the king begot Solomon...
> Matthan begot Jacob. And Jacob begot Joseph, the husband of Mary,
> and of her was born Jesus who is called Christ.
> **St. Matthew 1:1-16**

Then how do we explain the genealogy given in the Gospel of St. Luke? If we read his account Joseph is still a descendent of King David but his father is not Jacob:

> ... Joseph, the son of Heli, the son of Matthat, the son of Levi...
> **St. Luke 3:23**

Who was right? Both of them. Now you ask, "How could Joseph have two fathers?" This is how: Heli, also known as Joachim, was Mary's father. According to Levitic law, upon marrying the Virgin Mary, Joseph's "legal father" or "father in-law" became Heli (Joachim).

If you notice in Matthew's account, the word "begot" is used when descending the family tree, which means that they were biological fathers or at least loving guardians thought to be fathers. In St. Luke's account, the words "son of" are used instead of "begot." This would refer to "son in the eyes of the law," our modern day "son in-law."

Back then, who you were in the eyes of the law mattered a great deal, especially when it came to inheriting land and goods from your wife's father. When Joseph wed Mary, he became the legal son of Heli (Joachim) and therefore was included in the inheritance.

In the scriptures we are not given any details of Joseph's childhood or his early manhood, so we have to look to other sources for even a glimpse of Joseph before he appears in the Holy Bible. In the seventeenth century, a Spanish nun named Maria de Agreda was given heavenly insights into the life of the Holy Family which were compiled into four monumental volumes. Her book *Mystical City of God* has been acclaimed by Popes and theologians, and she has since been declared Venerable by the Church. Here is what was revealed to her concerning Joseph:

> [1]He was to be a miracle of holiness...
> He was sanctified in his mother's womb seven months after his conception,
> and the leaven of sin was destroyed in him for the whole course of his life.
> The holy child Joseph was born most beautiful and perfect of body
> and caused in his parents ... an extraordinary delight,
> ... The child began to know God by faith,
> [and] he eagerly listened and understood profoundly all that was
> taught him in regard to God and his works.

> He was of a kind disposition, loving, affable, and growing in virtue and

> perfection
> and advancing toward his espousal with most holy Mary
> by an altogether irreproachable life.
>
> In the virtue and perfection of chastity
> the holy spouse was elevated higher than the seraphim;
> for the purity, which they possessed *without* body,
> St. Joseph possessed *in* his earthly body and mortal flesh;
> **Mystical City of God**
> **Book 5, Chapter 4**

It makes sense that God infused into Joseph many virtues and graces in order to fully live the Gospel that Jesus was later to announce to the world. Joseph surpassed even the highest order of angels when it came to sanctity. The angels are pure without body, but Joseph, on the other hand, was pure while still *in* a human body! If I had been able to choose my father before I was born and had the power to make him saintly and pure of body and mind, I would have. I would have granted him special favours before he even knew me. Why would I have done this? Out of love and honour for the role of father, which in time he would fulfill. The same goes for the Virgin Mary. If I could have chosen my mother and made her pure of body and mind and without stain of original sin, I would have. Who wouldn't? Anyone who says that they would not is either lying, or crazy! God did this for his earthly parents before they even knew each other. God did this out of love, as this was His most special gift, reserved especially for them.

    In all, there were forty generations from Abraham to Jesus Christ. Joseph was a descendent of great patriarchs, princes, and kings, and when Jesus chose Joseph to be his father on earth, he too became linked with this royal lineage.

    This fulfills the Old Testament prophecies from the Book of the Prophet Isaiah:

> " ... a shoot will sprout from the stump of Jesse,
> and from his roots a bud will blossom. The Spirit of the Lord
> will rest upon him: A Spirit of Wisdom, a Spirit of Counsel
> and of Strength and of Fear of the Lord ... Not by appearances
> shall he judge ... but he shall judge the poor with justice ...
> Justice shall be his waistband and faithfulness a belt upon his hips."
> **Isaiah 11:1-5**

> "Fear not, O Jacob ... I will pour out My Spirit upon your offspring,
> and My blessing upon your descendents.
> ... One shall say, 'I am the Lord's,' another shall
> be named after Jacob, and this one will write on his hand,
> 'The Lord's' and Israel will be his surname."
> **Isaiah 44:2-5**

So why wasn't Joseph meant to have the crown? He had a perfect claim to the throne, but with what army would he defeat the foreign king who sat on his throne? And besides, what was God's will in all this? We read the words of Jacob in the Book of Genesis, who prophesied about this:

> "The sceptre shall not depart from Judea ...
> until He comes to whom it belongs.
> To Him will be the obedience of nations."
> **Genesis 49:10**

This prophecy says that the kingdom will be taken away from God's chosen people when the arrival of Jesus Christ is at hand. The loss of the Davidic crown was the sign of the coming of the Redeemer. This removal of authority happened at the time when Joseph was born into the world, to be the herald of the Lord who was to come shortly and proclaim the Kingdom of God. This kingdom would surpass those of the earthly realm and Christ would be its king. Joseph was meant to serve the Lord as a worker and to hide and humble himself in domestic –life—therefore sanctifying it and giving dignity to an honest day's work. This he did for the greater glory of God.

Imagine Joseph working hard during the day, sweat dripping off his brow as he fought to make ends meet. Imagine him lying in bed at night, pondering life and its meaning. Did he ever wonder what life would be like if he were king? He had a claim to the throne and yet here he was, a labourer, making his living by working with his hands. Did he dream of living in the palace with throngs of servants and visiting dignitaries? Did he imagine his beautiful bride, full of virtue and grace? How did he picture her? She would sit next to him at the royal table, her beauty the talk of all the people. They would have banquets in halls of gold and precious stones and entertain friends till dawn. The tables would glisten with gold plates and ornaments, overflowing with fresh fruit and nuts. Musicians would play a constant stream of melodies, filling the royal air that surrounded them. Sweet perfumes and lovely dancers, wine in abundance, entertainers and exotic birds to serenade them when all was finished. Imagine this splendour and luxury! Imagine all the wealth! He would never have to do manual labour again! Imagine Joseph being the envy of everyone! Imagine Joseph waking up. Yes, this would all have been a dream, but in actuality would he really have wanted all this? No.

> The covetous man is never satisfied with money,
> and the lover of wealth reaps no fruit from it;
> ... Where there are great riches, there are also many to devour them.
> Of what use are they to the owner except to feast his eyes upon?
> Sleep is sweet to the labouring man, whether he eats little or much,
> but the rich man's abundance allows him no sleep.
> **Sirach 5:9-12**

Joseph's humility exalted him above all his noble ancestors and made him great in the sight of God. Joseph did indeed have royal blood flowing through his veins, but he lived like an average Jewish man. He lived like an "average Joe." No palace, no power, no crown. And this was fine with him because he enjoyed his life and felt blessed to have what he did. In him, the Lord was preparing a true friend, and just as Jesus chose some of His apostles from among the lowly, He too chose His father. When Christ gives us the Beatitudes, surely we see Joseph as one of the blessed in God's eyes:

> "Blessed are the poor in spirit, for theirs is the kingdom of Heaven.
> Blessed are the meek, for they shall possess the earth.
> ... Blessed are the merciful, for they shall obtain mercy.
> Blessed are the clean of heart, for they shall see God.
> ... Rejoice and exult, because your reward is great in Heaven!"
> **St. Matthew 5:3-12**

The Just Man
Chapter 2: the Scent of Wood

> ... And I saw that there is nothing better for a man
> than to rejoice in his work.
> **Ecclesiastes 3:22**

We know from the Bible that Joseph was a just man with a humble demeanour. He made an honest living as a tradesman and no doubt was a great friend to others—always willing to extend a helping hand. We are told that Joseph was a carpenter, one who works with wood. We picture the scene at his workshop with people coming in and out. We see curled wood shavings carpeting the floor and little piles of sawdust scattered throughout his shop. We hear the rhythmic sawing of wood, constant like a heartbeat. To some this would be considered "noise," but to Joseph this is music. He makes his work into an art and puts every effort into each piece he –makes—whether it be a table, a bed, or even a plough. To him a quiet workshop is an idle one. "Noise" means there is work being done. Work being done means there is food on the table.

But did Joseph work only with wood? The word "faber," used in the Latin scriptures when defining Joseph's occupation, was a general term applied to a workman in any material; this could be one who works with wood, stone, iron, or even precious metals. St. Hilarion, St. Isidore, and St. Bede believed that Joseph was an ironsmith and wrote in their commentaries on the Gospels that Jesus was the son of "the smith who subdues iron with fire." The great saints Justin Martyr, Thomas Aquinas, and John Chrysostom, however, held the opinion that Joseph was in fact a worker of wood, as was Jesus:

> Jesus came to John, being reputed the son of Joseph,
> the *carpenter*, or *worker in wood*, and He Himself was reckoned to be a
> *carpenter*; for while He dwelt amongst men He had performed
> *carpenter's work*,
> making ploughs and yokes, teaching us to live just lives free from idleness.
> **St. Justin Martyr,**
> *Dialogue With Trypho*

> Jesus was reputed to be the son of Joseph,
> who was not a forger of iron but a *worker in wood*.
> **St. Thomas Aquinas,**
> ***In Reference Matthew 13***

> Therefore was Mary espoused to a *carpenter*,
> because Jesus, the Spouse of the Church, was to work,
> the salvation of the world by the wood of the Cross.
> **St. John Chrysostom,**
> ***Expounding Matthew's Gospel***

The accepted idea is that Joseph *was* a carpenter who worked with wood, but also worked with other materials on the side. The earliest art depicting Joseph shows him holding carpentry tools, but we are allowed to picture him working with both wood *and* iron; he made chests, cradles, beds, buckets, doors, and cabinets and pieces requiring iron such as cartwheels (which had iron hubs), sickles, and knives. Also, he could be called on to help fix up a neighbour's house by shaping thick planks for reinforcing houses, replacing locks, or hanging doors. What Joseph did for a living isn't as important as *how* he did it! Certainly, Joseph was known as being not only a fine workman, but also a man of integrity. The people of Nazareth knew that they could trust him to do the best job he could and at the same time not overcharge them. Their satisfaction in his work was his –pride—but not to the point of vanity. Joseph was a master of his trade and put care into the work he did for people, and the people of Nazareth knew this. They knew that he was a good man who was proud of what he was and put his love into everything he did.

> Watch, stand fast in the faith, act like men, be strong.
> Let all that you do be done in love.
> **1 Corinthians 16:13-14**

> The clang of the hammer deafens his ears,
> his eyes are fixed on [what] he is shaping.
> His care is to finish his work, and he keeps watch till he perfects it in detail.
> ... [He] maintain[s] God's ancient handiwork, and [his] concern
> is for exercise of [his] skill.
> **Sirach 38:28, 34**

He could have been a baker, a merchant, a goldsmith, or even a carpenter but *how* he laboured is what matters. Does Joseph give dignity to work and work to him? *Yes!* Did he put all his effort into his work? *Yes!* Was he sanctified by his work? *Yes!* He offered his work to God, and he did it with honour and love! Work is a means to sanctification! Though his hands are rough and calloused, he has the tenderest of hearts.

> There is nothing better for man than to eat and drink
> and provide himself with good things by his labours.
> Even this, I realized, *is from the hand of God*.
> **Ecclesiastes 2:24**

The Just Man
Chapter 3: Love Ordained

> Be you, therefore, imitators of God,
> as very dear children and walk in love ... Husbands, love your wives...
> Even thus ought husbands also to love their wives as their own bodies.
> He who loves his own wife, loves himself;
> and let the wife respect her husband.
> **Ephesians 5:25-33**

The word "Love" appears more than sixty times in the Holy Bible, but how many of us have attached meaning to this word? We say it constantly, throwing it around at this person or that person, this thing or that thing. I love you! I love this song! I love Portuguese food! We need to understand the deeper meaning of the word "Love," as it is used in the Bible only when it is genuine and real. There are two different kinds of love in the Bible. The first and greatest love of all is God's love for each and every one of us, which ultimately saves us:

> For God so loved the world that He gave His only-begotten Son,
> that those who believe in Him may not perish,
> but may have life everlasting.
> **St. John 3:16**

The second type of love, which also comes from our Heavenly Father, is love for one another:

> Beloved, let us love one another, for love is from God.
> And everyone who loves is born of God, and knows God.
> ... If we love one another, God abides in us
> and His love is perfected in us.
> **1 St. John 4:7, 4:12**

Since God is love itself, we can marvel at how much Joseph and Mary must have loved each other and how they still do in the glory of Heaven. Joseph must have been smitten by her beauty and humility, and she must have felt the same for him. Surely, the house Jesus was to grow up in would be a house filled with love beyond measure, beyond anything we could comprehend.

It is not known for sure how Joseph and Mary came to be man and wife, but we are certain that their marriage was ordained by Heaven. God does not leave things to chance. Given the customs at the time, Mary was believed to be no older than sixteen when she was married. Joseph would have been anywhere from his late teens but no older than his mid-thirties. Through the ages, art has shown him as an elderly man hunched over his walking stick, barely able to stand. Joseph was not a senior citizen! No offence to the elderly, but God would choose a strong, energetic man who would be able to support his family. In the earliest depictions of Joseph, he is pictured as young and even beardless. For example, in the catacombs of Priscilla in the Via Salaria, on a third century tomb, he is shown as an upright young man without a beard. Why, then, was Joseph depicted as an old man in so much European art through the centuries?

There are two reasons for this, both of which are *false*, and which tend to tarnish Joseph's image.

The first reason was to explain the "brothers and sisters" of the Lord, mentioned in the Bible. The apocryphal book titled, "The History of the Carpenter Joseph," states that he was once a priest and a carpenter who was a widower with four sons and two daughters, meaning Mary's stepchildren would be far older then she was. Apparently, Joseph was old enough to be Mary's grandfather. This is *false*, and the notion of Christ having "brothers and sisters" is explained below in Chapter Eight, though some Christians are prejudiced and *do not want* an explanation and choose to be deaf to the fact that Mary and Joseph were virgins.

> He begot for himself four sons, and two daughters.
> Judas, Justus, James, and Simon. The names of the two daughters were
> Assia and Lydia.
> At length, the wife of the righteous Joseph, intent on the
> divine glory in all her works departed this life.
> **The History of the Carpenter Joseph 2**

The second reason for the elderly Joseph was to protect the virginity of Mary. The idea of the Virgin Mary living with a handsome and robust man was not acceptable as people would think that he might have some inclination to have sex with her, therefore robbing her of her virginal title. This insults both Joseph and his bride, not because sex is a bad thing, but because it places doubt in what Holy Scripture tells us. It is *false*. The Bible tells us that the Messiah would be born of a virgin. Mary herself tells us this when the angel Gabriel tells her she will conceive: "How can this be since I am a virgin?" The earliest saints of the Church, who would have had contact with the original twelve Apostles, were all in agreement that the mother of Jesus was a virgin both before and after the birth of Christ. Also, ancient Church traditions fully support that Mary and Joseph, by interior impulse to offer everything about themselves to God, had made vows of chastity early in life.

> ... [Mary] herself had made to the Lord a vow of virginity,
> which she would never violate by any intercourse with a man
> **Apocryphal Book of the Nativity of Mary 7**

> Gabriel was sent from God to a town of Galilee called Nazareth,
> to a virgin betrothed to a man named Joseph ...
> and the virgin's name was Mary.
> **St. Luke 1:26-28**

> How exalted in this virtue of virginity must Joseph have been,
> who was destined by the Eternal Father to be the
> companion in virginity of Mary!
> Both had made a vow to preserve virginity for their entire lives,
> and it was the Will of God to join them in the bond of a holy marriage ...
> **St. Francis de Sales, *Entretien Spirituels***

This was not a common practice; however, Jesus was not a common man, so why should we doubt His parents' uncommon vows? Joseph and Mary were Jews, and yes, it was unusual to make vows of virginity in their culture, but it is the same in our own culture today!

If someone tells you they have made a vow of virginity, would you doubt them? Probably not, because who would lie about something like that? You wouldn't doubt them, but you would be inclined to ask them why they chose to do this. Why would anyone want to live without sex!? Because sex, in its proper context of "making love," is one of life's most beautiful treasures, and some people, impelled to serve God in a unique way, choose to offer it to the Lord instead of to themselves. They are giving the most beautiful gift they can offer to God. Virginity in our culture is seen as prudishness and "old school," and some people lie to say that they are *not* virgins! The Bible gives us many examples of people who gave their gift of virginity to God and were not ashamed of people knowing it. They were seen as holy, not because sex is bad and they were abstaining from it, but because they saw this gift as being so wonderful and they wanted to offer the gift and themselves to God. It is a selfless act of love!

> And I saw, and behold, the Lamb
> was standing upon Mount Sion, and with Him
> a hundred and forty-four thousand having his name
> and the name of his Father written on their foreheads.
> ... These are they who were not [known] with women; for they are virgins.
> **Revelation 14:1, 14:4**

The great St. Gregory Nazianzen proclaimed that the first virgin ever is the Holy Trinity. God the Father is a virgin who generates the Son in all His goodness; God the Son is a virgin who existed in Heaven without a mother; God the Holy Spirit is a virgin, who proceeds gloriously from the Father and the Son. As the Heavenly Trinity is the first and altogether virgin, so is the second Trinity, on earth. If Jesus is a virgin and Mary is a virgin, why wouldn't Joseph, who completes this virginal Trinity, be one as they are? Jesus is the Head of the virgins! Mary is the mother of virgins! Joseph is the guardian and patron of virgins!

There are two traditional beliefs about how the betrothal between Joseph and Mary came to be. The first belief being that their marriage was arranged by their parents. Plain and simple. The second is a little more interesting. The Fathers and Doctors of the Church generally agree that God Himself pointed out Joseph as the man who would wed the Virgin. St. Epiphanius and St. Gregory, for example, believed that Mary's husband was chosen by lot. For example, when the Apostles were trying to find a replacement for Judas Iscariot, the man who betrayed Christ, they gathered and prayed to God for a sign of who was to be chosen and they drew lots between them.

> And they prayed and said,
> "Thou, Lord, who knows the hearts of all,
> show us which of these two men you have chosen ..."
> And they drew lots between them and the lot fell upon Matthias;
> **Acts 1:24-26**

There were gathered a group of young men of the House of David, Joseph among them, who wanted Mary as their wife. Many Church Fathers believed that in order to find a suitable husband for her, the High Priest Zachary, with divine inspiration, recalled how the Israelites rebelled against Moses and Aaron.

In order to convince the Israelites that Aaron was the chosen High Priest, God said to Moses:

> "Speak to the Israelites and get one staff from each of them ...
> Mark each man's name on his staff; and mark Aaron's name ...
> Then lay them down
> in the Meeting Tent, ... There the staff of the man of My choice will sprout."
> ... The next day, when Moses entered the Tent,
> Aaron's staff ... had sprouted and put forth not only shoots,
> but blossoms as well, and even bore ripe almonds.
> **Numbers 17:1-23**

So using this example, Zachary told each of the men of the House of David to bring a rod with his name written on it, and the man whose rod blossomed would be the husband of Mary. Of course it was Joseph's rod that blossomed. This scene was related in a few apocryphal books such as the Gospel of Pseudo-Matthew, which was not incorporated into the Holy Bible, and would be seen as fulfilling the prophecy of Isaiah.

> "... a shoot will sprout from the stump of Jesse,
> and from his roots a bud will blossom.
> The Spirit of the Lord will rest upon him ..."
> **Isaiah 11:1-5**

> "Therefore all the unmarried descendants of David were brought together ...
> and each presented his staff ... When no man's staff flowered ...
> Joseph then brought forth his staff which immediately blossomed with lilies
> and the Holy Spirit perched
> upon it in the form of a dove. In this way, Joseph was chosen by God
> to be the husband of Mary."
> **The Gospel of Pseudo-Matthew**

This tradition is still upheld by many Christians to this day and a great deal of art shows Joseph pictured with a staff blooming lilies or just the flowers themselves as a reminder of both his worthiness and purity in the eyes of the Heavenly Father.

Imagine how honoured Joseph would have felt to be the chosen one. Out of all these men, some more successful than he, God chose a humble worker. Think of how happy and yet nervous he would have been when seeing the young virgin. Think of the innocent awkwardness of Joseph and Mary when they first encountered each other alone, in order to get to know each other. They would *both* have been nervous because they had *both* made vows of virginity to the Lord. Mary would have told Joseph this in order to be completely honest with him. He should not expect to have sexual relations with her and therefore, she could not bear him children.

If he wanted, he could find a more suitable wife who had *not* made this vow to the Lord. Joseph however, was relieved at hearing these words! He too had made a vow to the Lord to remain a virgin! How perfect a union this would be! They would be able to support each other in their vows and be strong for one another! Once the tension was over they began to share their hopes, dreams, and fears. How God must have infused into their hearts a love so beautiful and holy for one another! How they must have thanked God that He chose to bring them to live out their lives together in His service! In Mary, God has given Joseph the perfect bride and the Book of Proverbs describes who this bride is:

> ...her value is far beyond pearls.
> Her husband, entrusting his heart to her, has an unfailing prize!
> She brings him good, and not evil... She reaches out her hands to the poor, and extends her arms to the needy. Her husband is prominent ... She is clothed with strength and dignity and she laughs at the days to come. She opens her mouth in wisdom, and on her tongue is kindly counsel ...
> "Many are the women of proven worth,
> but you have excelled them all"
> **Proverbs 31:10-29**

When we read the beautiful Nuptial Ode, in the Book of Psalms, we can easily envision Mary saying to her beloved:

> "My heart overflows with a goodly theme as I sing my ode ...
> Fairer in beauty are you than the sons of men;

grace is poured out upon your lips; thus God has blessed you forever ...
You love justice ... therefore God ... has anointed you with the oil of gladness above your ... kings!"
Psalm 45:2-8

And Joseph serenades his bride:

"All glorious is the ... daughter as she enters;
her raiment is threaded with spun gold.
In embroidered apparel she is borne in...
Behind her the virgins of her train ... are borne in with gladness and joy;
... I will make your name memorable through all generations;
therefore shall nations praise you forever and ever!"
Psalm 45:14-17

The Just Man
Chapter Four: The Messenger

> "And thou shalt have joy and gladness,
> and many will rejoice ..."
> **St. Luke 1:14**

After Mary and Joseph were betrothed to one another, the date of their marriage was set, according to church tradition, for January 23. It was between the betrothal or *quiddushin,* and the actual marriage ceremony, *nissu'in,* we believe, that the Archangel Gabriel paid homage to the Virgin Mary:

> "Hail, full of grace, the Lord is with you!
> Blessed are you among women!"
> When she heard him she was troubled at his word,
> and kept pondering what manner of greeting this was.
> **St. Luke 1:28-29**

We picture Mary as slightly frightened at the moment the angel arrives, but as his message to her unfolds, she is more amazed than scared:

> "Do not be afraid, Mary, for you have found grace with God.
> Behold, you will conceive ... and will bring forth a son;
> and you will call his name Jesus. He will be great, and will be called
> the Son of the Most High; and the Lord God
> will give Him the throne of David...
> and of His kingdom there will be no end!"
> **St. Luke 1:30-33**

"There is no way people are going to believe this!" she thinks to herself. Not only did an angel visit her to tell her that she had found favour with God, but also that she was to bring His Son into the world! A humble Jewish girl giving birth to the Son of God when she herself was a virgin? What would people think? What would Joseph think? "Nobody will believe me," she sighs in her heart. So she works up the courage to ask the angel how this will happen, not doubting his words, but just wanting more information. This was a big deal! Gabriel answers her:

> "The Holy Spirit will come upon you and the power
> of the Most High will overshadow you; and therefore the Holy One
> to be born will be called the Son of God."
> **St. Luke 1:35-36**

Mary is feeling mixed emotions as she is filled with a sense of honour and humility. She wonders what she has done to deserve this favour with the Lord as she feels unworthy to even have a visit from an angel, let alone to be called "full of grace." Did she wonder why God chose her as His beloved? And, at the words of Gabriel, did she make the connection with the Old Testament prophecy that a young virgin would conceive and bear a son?

So many questions, but she feels comforted and accepts the Will of God. She answers the angel simply:

> "Behold the handmaid of the Lord;
> be it done to me as you say."
> **St. Luke 1:38**

Mary, full of love and thanks for the great things that God has done, is moved to praise Him and glorify Him as she exclaims her "Magnificat" in the presence of her cousin Elizabeth:

> "My soul magnifies the Lord,
> and my spirit rejoices in God my Saviour;
> because He has regarded the lowliness of His handmaid;
> for behold, ... all generations will call me blessed;
> because He who is mighty has done great things for me,
> and holy is His Name!
> He has ... exalted the lowly ... He has given help to Israel."
> **St. Luke 1:46-54**

During the period of time between the engagement and the marriage, Joseph busied himself with his work because soon he would be supporting his wife. Between praising God and thoughts of the lovely Mary, Joseph had little else on his mind other than preparing for their future. As the time drew closer,

Joseph was even more earnest in his anticipation, and his happiness was marked clearly on his face as he radiated joy to others. All was going well for him, until one day:

> "...before they came together [married],
> she was found to be with child ... "
> **St. Matthew 1:18**

Yes, Joseph found out that his virgin bride was with child, but not just any child, the very Son of God! His humble little wife was to be the mother of the Saviour and she wanted him to be the father. Joseph wanted what was best for her, yet he didn't know if he could take her as his wife anymore. Did he doubt her story? Eastern Church tradition says that Joseph was tempted by the devil at first, being told that Mary was indeed an adulteress and that Joseph was a fool for believing her. The Devil tries to convince Joseph to abandon Mary, therefore interfering with God's ultimate plan. This temptation of Joseph is depicted in many Nativity icons as he is shown being approached by the Devil who is disguised as an elderly shepherd. Joseph did not doubt the words of his bride, but he had to fight with the actuality of what she was saying to him. He felt unworthy to even be considered to raise this Holy Child. The Virgin Mary would need someone more competent and well-off to take care of her and the child. It was a great deal of pressure on the man. Mary was going to be an instrument of the Most High, and he didn't feel like he could handle the great responsibility of being the proper husband and father. What should he do about this? Joseph wasn't anyone special, how could he take on this great task, which was so important to the world? He thought about divorcing Mary so that she could find a man more worthy of this. He simply did not feel adequate. "The Son of God must have a better father than I would be," he thought to himself. He also thought about the law: if a woman was suspected of committing adultery, she was put to shame in public and later stoned to death. He knew that she was still a virgin, but would the Law believe it? He could never let this happen to her because he loved her so much. She was his one and only beloved.

It was time for him to make the hardest decision of his life: to send Mary away quietly to spare her dignity and her life.

> Joseph her husband, being a just man,
> and not wanting to expose her to reproach,
> was minded to put her away privately.
> **St. Matthew 1:19**

No doubt this would have caused both Joseph and Mary a lot of heartache and despair. Was their marriage not ordained by God? What of the miracle that announced their engagement? So many thoughts, full of confusion, must have swarmed through his head as Joseph called out in anguish to the heavens. We hear him cry out to the night sky:

> "Hear, O Lord, the sound of my call!
> Have pity on me, and answer me!
> Of You my heart speaks; You my glance seeks;
> Your presence, O Lord, I seek. Hide not Your face from me!
> Do not in anger repel Your servant. You are my Helper ...
> forsake me not, O God, my Saviour!"
> **[3]Psalm 26:7-9**

Mary must have wept at night as she gazed up at the same starry sky, asking God to make things right. Asking God to take pity on Joseph, and to enlighten him to ease his suffering. God Himself felt deep sorrow at seeing Joseph so distraught and so the Lord, being full of mercy and compassion, sent Gabriel once again to deliver a message.

> But while he thought on these things, behold,
> an angel of the Lord appeared to him in a dream, saying,
> "Do not be afraid, Joseph, son of David, to take to thee Mary thy wife,
> for that which is conceived in her is of the Holy Spirit.
> And she will bring forth a son, and you will call him Jesus;
> for He shall save His people from their sins!"
> **St. Matthew 1:20-22**

> 'O Joseph, why art thou minded to put away Mary thy wife?
> Know that whatsoever hath been wrought in her
> hath all been done by the will of God.
> The virgin shall bring forth a son, whom thou shall call by the name Jesus;
> ... He shall come with great power, which God shall give him, and shall work great miracles, whereby many shall be saved'. Joseph, arising from

> sleep, gave thanks to God, and abode with Mary all his life,
> serving God with all sincerity.
> **Apocryphal Book of Barnabas 2:1**

Incredible! Joseph too had seen the angel! And heard the message! He experienced the same event as his beloved! He had his own Annunciation! What a relief! With this dream the angel not only confirmed to Joseph that Mary was indeed with child by the power of the Holy Spirit, but that this child would one day save people from their sins! Also, Joseph is bestowed with the high honour of not only naming the boy "Jesus," which means "God Saves," but also raising the Son of the Most High as if He were his own son! God is telling him that *he is worthy*! God has given him the grace necessary to take on this important life! Joseph found favour with the Lord! God Himself wants Joseph for a father! The angel tells Joseph to have no fear and to take Mary as his wife, and assume the legitimate rights and position of true father and true husband. God wants him specifically! Not the rich guy on the hill, not the noble warrior, but the lowly worker.

In the Old Testament, we are given a similar story involving the highly revered forefather Abraham. The message is the same but the circumstances are different. Abraham is told that his ninety-year-old wife will conceive and bear a child in her old age, who was to become the great man Isaac:

> And as Abraham fell prostrate, he laughed and said to himself,
> "Shall a son be born to the one who is a hundred years old?
> Shall Sara who is ninety bear a child?
> **Genesis 17:17**

Just as unlikely that a hundred-year-old man and his ninety-year-old wife would conceive and have a child born to them, so too was it impossible for a virgin to conceive. However, unlike father Abraham who laughed at this notion, Joseph the Humble accepted the message that was entrusted to him. He might not have completely understood how this was to be, but for him it did not matter. What mattered was his complete trust in God and the utter surrender to His Divine Will.

> "Therefore, take these words of mine into your heart and soul.
> Bind them at your wrist as a sign and let them
> be a pendant on your forehead."
> **Deuteronomy 11:18**

As soon as the dream was over, he got up and went straight to Mary to tell her the news. God has not abandoned him after all! He apologized to Mary and said that he would indeed be her husband and protector and that he was honoured to have her for his wife, and to have the child within her as his son. He held her and reaffirmed his love and commitment to her and the unborn child.

"Ah, you are beautiful, my beloved,
ah, you are beautiful; your eyes are doves!
... As a lily among thorns, so is my beloved among women.
... You are beautiful, my beloved, and there is no blemish in you.
You are an enclosed garden ... a fountain sealed.
You are a garden fountain, a well of water flowing fresh!
... [You] come forth like the dawn, as beautiful as the moon,
as resplendent as the sun ... how beautiful you are,
how pleasing, my love, my delight!"
Canticles of Canticles
1:15, 2:2, 4:7-15, 6:10, 7:7

And the Holy Virgin replied to her husband:

"As an apple tree among the trees if the woods,
so is my [beloved] among men. I delight to rest in his shadow ...
He brings me into the banquet hall and his emblem over me is love.
... Strengthen me ... for I am faint with love!
His left hand is under my head and his right arm embraces me.
My [beloved] is radiant ... he stands out among thousands!
His eyes are like doves beside running waters.
... his stature is like the trees on Lebanon, imposing as cedars.
His mouth is sweetness itself; he is all delight.
Such is my [beloved], and such my friend."
Canticles of Canticles
2:3-6, 5:10–16

"Joseph teaches us that it is possible to love without possessing ...
In contemplating Joseph, all men and women can, by God's grace, come to experience healing from their emotional wounds, if only they embrace the plan that God has begun to bring about in those close to him, just as Joseph entered into the work of redemption through Mary and as a result of what God had already done in her."
Pope Benedict XVI
Yaoundé, Cameroon, March 18, 2009

The Just Man
Chapter 5: The Garden

> You are an enclosed garden...
> You are a park that puts forth pomegranates,
> with all choice fruits; nard and saffron, calamus and cinnamon,
> with all kinds of incense; myrrhs and aloes, with all the finest spices.
> I have come to my garden ... I gather my myrrh and my spices,
> I eat my honey and my sweetmeats, I drink my wine and my milk.
> Eat friends; drink! Drink freely of love!
> **Canticles of Canticles 4:12-15, 5:1**

Joseph was familiar with the writings of the Old Testament and, knowing that Jesus would one day save humanity, he must have reflected on the Book of Genesis where mankind first became in need of saving. For the Jewish people, Eve had an essential role in God's First Covenant. It was Eve who was the mother of mankind, but it was also she who was led astray by the serpent in the Garden of Eden. She gave in to temptation and ate of the forbidden fruit, and since this event, all her descendents were stained with what is known as "original sin." At this time, God was already planning a new and everlasting Covenant, which would be the salvation of all. He was going to send forth a Second Adam and a Second Eve. Just as Eve was formed from Adam's rib, the New Adam was to be formed from a woman. This Eve was to be the mother of the New Adam who would crush the serpent who had deceived the world:

> "I will put enmity between you and the woman,
> between your seed and her seed; he shall crush your head,
> and you will lie in wait for his heel."
> **Genesis 3:15**

Joseph was delighted to know that the time had come for the words of Scripture to begin their fulfillment. He wondered, was Mary the woman mentioned by God in the Garden of Eden? Yes! It was all clear now! Everything was beginning to make sense: his wife, Mary, was the New Eve to mankind. The seed of the woman mentioned in Genesis is the Word Made –Flesh—Jesus – Christ—the New Adam and His followers! This New Adam, brought forth by the New Eve, would redeem the world and bring about new life, in contrast to the death brought on by the disobedience in the garden.

The writings of early Church Fathers give us evidence that the notion of Mary as the New Eve has roots in ancient Christianity. St. Justin Martyr (*circa* A.D. 120-165) compared the transgression and disobedience of Eve to the humility and obedience of Mary. Also, sometime between A.D. 180 and 240, Tertullian wrote this concerning the two women mentioned in the garden:

> "For unto Eve as yet a virgin,
> had crept the word ... 'death';
> equally into a virgin was to be introduced the Word of God,
> which was the builder-up of life."
> **Tertullian[4]**

There have already been comparisons made between Adam and Eve and Jesus Christ and His mother Mary, but what about Joseph? We know that Jesus is the New Adam and Mary the New Eve, but how, if at all, does Joseph fit into this picture of a "New Eden"? Let's start off by discussing the Holy Family in a different "Eden" comparison.

We can say that not only is Mary the New Eve to mankind, but she is also the Garden of Eden itself. Mary represents all that is good within this garden. She is the fertile soil, the lush green grass, and the fresh blossoms that perfume the air. She is the Mystical Rose of –God—His most pure, mortal creature. This Garden of Eden, personified by the Virgin Mary, is the City of God on earth! She is inviting and welcoming with open arms for the human race and is maternal towards all of God's children and wants us to share in what God has given her. She is the Golden –City—the bountiful Garden of Eden!

> The Lord God planted a garden in Eden...
> [He] made to grow out of the ground
> all kinds of trees pleasant to the sight
> and good for food ...
> **Genesis 2:8-10**

> Glorious things are said of you, O City of God!
> ... One and all were born in her;
> and He who has established her
> is the Most High Lord!
> **Psalm 87:3-5**

There is something special about the –garden—something special about Mary, but for some time that something special was hidden from us. Enclosed within the garden, in the midst of all the splendour and beauty, grows a sapling. This humble sapling grows within the garden and becomes the most beautiful of all plants. It develops and grows into a mighty tree and comes to be known as the Tree of Life, whose fruits would change the course of history forever!

> The Lord God made grow out of the ground...
> the Tree of Life also in the midst of the garden ...
> **Genesis 2:9-10**

> And he showed me a river of the water of life, clear as crystal,
> coming forth from the throne of God and of the lamb.
> In the midst of the city street ... was the Tree of Life,
> bearing twelve fruits ... and leaves for the healing of the nations.
> ... Blessed are they who wash their robes that they may have
> the right to the Tree of Life,
> and that by the gates they may enter into the city.
> **Revelation 22:1-2, 14**

We are saved by this wood, which is our crib, our cross, and our Christ! Jesus is the Tree of Life, which grows in His mother Mary, the true paradise of Eden.

> How lovely is Your dwelling place,
> O Lord of Hosts! My soul yearns ...
> My heart and my flesh cry out for the living God!
> **Psalm 84:2-4**

After the fall of man the gates to this paradise on earth were closed, so as to guard Eden and what flourished within. At the gates God placed a cherub with a sword of fire to protect the purity and sanctity of the –garden—to protect Mary and the Holy Child that grew within her. When people think of the cherubim they picture cute little angels who fly around without a care in their

heads, playing music and dancing. This, however, is not what was protecting Eden. The baby angels are actually known as *putti*, not cherubim. A cherub is, in actuality, a little more intimidating. The Book of Ezekiel describes what the cherubim
look like:

>Each had four faces and four wings;
>something like human hands were under their wings.
>... Each had four faces: the first face was that of an ox,
>the second that of a man, the third that of a lion,
>and the fourth that of an eagle.
>**Ezekiel 10:14**

>... at the east of the garden of Eden
>He placed the cherubim, and the flaming sword,
>which turned every way, to guard the way to the Tree of Life.
>**Genesis 3:24**

God entrusted the holy realm of Eden into Joseph's –hands—hands that felt unworthy, but always ready to do God's Will. Joseph is the cherub who shields the garden and what is contained within. He has a duty to protect what the Lord has given him, and he stands guard tirelessly on account of true love. True love for the God who finds in Joseph not only one who is humble enough, but also one who is worthy enough to carry out this task! True love for his wife who was predestined to carry the Saviour of the world in her womb! True love for the Holy Child within her who comes to the world not to condemn mankind, but to save us! He is protecting the –garden—the tabernacle in which the Tree of Life, Jesus Christ, is growing. Joseph loves his bride and the child within her so much that not only does he embrace them and shield them with his arms, but also with a sword of fire! His role is one that was reserved especially for him since before the dawn of time! This man, just as the cherub standing watch, is a soldier of the Lord!

>"O God, behold [your] shield,
>and look upon the face of your anointed ...
>I had rather lie at the threshold of the house of my God
>than to dwell in the tents of the wicked ...
>O Lord of Hosts, happy the [man] who trust[s] in You!"
>**Psalm 84:10-13**

The Just Man
Chapter 6: Road to Fatherhood

> When a man walks in integrity and justice,
> happy are his children after him!
> **Proverbs 20:7**

As time passed, Joseph and Mary lived a simple but happy life as they waited in joyful hope for the birth of their promised Son. Imagine how excited the couple would have been to announce that they were going to have a child! The conception of a child is great news to eager parents, and we can imagine how their friends and family rejoiced at the news! Joseph and Mary would have known that he wasn't the child's biological father, but that wouldn't keep him from being a *true* father. He would be excited, as most men would be, to tell the whole world that he was going to be a dad! Mary would marvel at Joseph's acceptance and anticipation of the child and she would be even more in love with him at seeing this. Joseph must have wanted to tell everyone that his virgin wife was to give birth to the Son of God and that God chose *him*, of all people, to be head of this Holy Family! But being humble and pure of heart, he kept these things to himself and no doubt pondered them in his heart, just as Mary did.

> "Blessed be the Lord, for He has heard the sound of [our] pleading;
> the Lord is [our] strength and [our] shield!
> In Him [our] hearts[s] trust, and [we] find help;
> then [our] heart[s] exult, and with [our] song
> [we] give Him thanks."
> **Psalm 28:6-7**

As the days went by, the Holy Child grew within His –tabernacle—the Virgin Mary's –womb—and His time was drawing near to enter this world. Mary held Joseph's hand flat against her belly as the child kicked for the first time, growing anxious for His own birth! Such amazement and wonder this unborn child had brought to them!

Then, a census was ordered by Caesar Augustus, which meant that everyone had to return to the lands of their forefathers to register. Joseph had to report to Bethlehem, the birthplace of King David, which is roughly 120 miles south of Nazareth, where he and Mary were living. To reach Bethlehem they would have to cross the rough terrain of Samaria into Judea. No doubt Joseph was hesitant to bring Mary along, since she was soon to give birth and needed to rest and keep comfortable, but Mary being the devoted wife that she was, desperately wanted to accompany her husband on this journey. During these times, travel was unsafe and was full of dangers such as the threat of wild animals and roadside thieves, and we think of how much harder it would be to make this trip with a nine months pregnant wife! Joseph and Mary most likely joined a caravan on their way to Bethlehem, so as to be safer.
This would have been a group of men, women, children, camels, and donkeys that would walk in the heat of day and –sleep—with one eye –open—at night.

This humble journey was the first Corpus Christi procession to take place, except the Body of Christ was enclosed in His mother's womb, rather than being exposed for veneration by the faithful. Mary's mantle was the canopy over the Hidden –Jesus—our Bread of –Life—and Joseph's sandal prints on the dusty earth were as palms laid out for the Lord to tread on.

And Joseph also went from Galilee out of the town of Nazareth
into Judea to the town of David, which is called Bethlehem ... to register,
together with Mary his wife, who was with child.
St. Luke 2:4-5

But you, Bethlehem ... too small to be among the clans of Judea,
from you shall come forth ... one who is to be ruler in Israel;
whose origin is from ... ancient times.
Micah 5:1-2

This journey on foot surely must have taken its toll on Joseph's feet, but with each step he took, he knew that he was moving closer to fulfilling what the angel had told him. Mary, being so devoted, gazed with admiration at the man who was her husband and protector. On the few stops they made to rest, we can imagine Mary humbly and quietly washing Joseph's sore feet as he gave in to exhaustion and slept. Joseph would never have asked her to do this or even let her if she offered, for she was so exalted in his eyes. We imagine Jesus awake in the womb as Mary does this and wonder if, by divine insight, He knew that one day He would do this same act for those He cared –for—a sign of humility and love. We know from the Bible that Jesus did this when He was older, as we are told in the Gospel of John:

> [He] rose up from the supper and laid aside His garments,
> and taking a towel, girded Himself. Then He poured water into the basin
> and began to wash the feet of the disciples, and to dry them with the towel...
> "Do you know what I have done to you? ... I, the Lord and Master, have
> washed your feet, you also ought to wash the feet of one another."
> **St. John 13:2-15**

Eventually, Mary and Joseph drew closer to their destination: Bethlehem, the town of David. The Holy Bible does not give us an account of this journey, but traditional roots in certain apocryphal books give us the thoughts and words of Joseph, followed by a prophetic vision seen by Mary as she rides the donkey:

> ... Joseph turned and saw that she was sad. And he said to himself, "Perhaps the child within her is troubling her."
> And shortly after, Joseph again turned around and saw her laughing, and said to her, "Mary, what has come upon thee?
> One moment thy face appears full of sadness and the next, full of joy?"
> **Infancy Book of James 17:6-8**

> ... Mary [answered] to Joseph,
> "I see two groups of people before me, the one weeping,
> and the other rejoicing"...
> For she saw the people of the Jews weeping,
> because they have departed from their God;
> and the people of the Gentiles rejoicing, because they have now been added
> and made near to the Lord, according to that which He promised
> to our fathers Abraham, Isaac, and Jacob:
> for the time is at hand when in the seed of Abraham
> all nations shall be blessed.
> **Book of Pseudo-Matthew 13:1**

Arriving in Bethlehem and searching for shelter during their stay, the holy couple were rejected by the innkeepers and residents. They should have left Nazareth days earlier in order to get a room. We sense that Joseph begins to feel desperate at not finding a place to stay. And to add to this, his lovely wife calmly told him: "It's time. He is coming."

Joseph panicked: "Now?! Are you sure!?"

Mary, trying to still keep her calm, answered: "Yes ... dear husband ... He is on His way".

Joseph felt overwhelmed and frantically knocked on every door he could.

Finally, he went to one last house and begged for help! The man apologized and stated that he too was out of room, and the only open spot is a cave out back, which the animals use. Joseph accepted the man's offer.

He felt relieved but also ashamed. He hung his head and looked at the ground as he told his wife that she would have to sleep in a cave with some animals for the night and that their Son would be born into this world not as babies are but as the lambs and calves are. When he looked at Mary, his eyes blurred as they swelled with tears and so he looked away. Mary smiled and reached for his hands, gently held them in hers, and reassured him that it didn't matter where they stayed, as long as they were together and with God. She reassured him that she loved him and that she was proud of him for all he had done. She reminded him that God was with them and would not forsake them. "Joseph, do not forget ...

> God is our refuge and strength, a very present help in trouble.
> Therefore we will not fear, though the earth be moved,
> and though the mountains be toppled into the depths of the sea;
> Though its waters rage and foam,
> and though the mountains tremble at its tumult.
> The Lord of Hosts is with us; the God of Jacob is our stronghold."
> **Psalm 46**

The Carpenter's Son
Chapter 7: A Humble Crib

> Humble yourself the more ... and you will find favour with God.
> For great is the power of God; by the humble he is glorified.
> **Sirach 3:18-20**

Joseph, with renewed strength, moved onwards to the cave. At the entrance, he shone his lantern to see what lay inside. A few sheep, some cows, and a pair of doves. He crept inside and searched for an ideal spot for Mary to lie down. In the far corner, there was a pile of straw, and for the most part it was pretty clean. He then went back to his wife and helped her down from the donkey's back. He unloaded all their belongings and made a bed out of straw with blankets stretched out over top. He then escorted Mary into her temporary bedchamber, and she assured him that this would do just fine. He helped her down onto the bed and gave her some water from their animal skin sack. Though up till now Mary had appeared very patient and calm, she began to sweat as her breathing pattern quickened. The Son of God was on His way! Humanity's greatest hero was about to come forth into our world to save us from our sins! Joseph didn't feel ready, there was still so much more he wanted to do to make the cave comfortable! But it would have to do as it was. Did Joseph panic as Mary gave birth to their Son? Was he calm and collected, holding his Virgin's hand as she pushed? A seldom asked question is, "Was Joseph even present at the moment of Christ's Birth?"

> Now, when the birth of the Lord was at hand,
> Joseph had gone away to seek midwives.
> And when he found them, he returned to the cave,
> and found with Mary the Infant, which she had brought forth.
> **Book of Pseudo-Matthew 13:3**

Though some apocryphal books state that Joseph was not present at the moment of Christ's delivery, this is very unlikely to be true. Joseph *was* present at the delivery of the Holy Child as God would not want him to miss the greatest moment of his life. Joseph was chosen by God to be His father on earth, and so it was Joseph who would be the first man to hold Holy Communion in his hands. He was the first to adore the Holy Eucharist in the form of the Divine Child as He came out from His human tabernacle, the Blessed Virgin. He held God in his arms! He wiped the Infant clean and kissed the face of God! He joyously proclaimed God's glory as he handed the Child to His mother. Joseph was, as most fathers would be, at this moment: anxious, joyful, and proud! His beloved had just given birth to the Saviour, a New Adam for the world! His wife had just given birth to Love Incarnate, their Son!

> ... she brought forth her firstborn son,
> and wrapped him in swaddling clothes,
> and laid him in a manger, because there was
> no room for them in the inn.
> **St. Luke 2:7**

> "I will bless her, and she shall be
> the mother of nations…"
> **Genesis 17:16**

> ... she was with child and she cried out in her pangs of birth.
> ... And she brought forth a male child, one who was to rule all the nations ...
> **Revelation 12:2, 5**

Words cannot truly express the magnitude of this event in history. This single moment, the bringing of this child into our world, means one thing to us, yet there are so many ways to describe what has just taken place. Salvation has just been given to us! Salvation is this child! Mary and Joseph no doubt heard the choirs of angels rejoicing at the birth! We imagine the night sky illuminated as if it were day, with the angels emanating light as they sing and dance! Salvation has come to mankind!

> And I heard as it were a voice of a great crowd,
> and as the voice of many waters,
> and as the voice of mighty thunders, saying,
> "Alleluia! ... Let us be glad and rejoice and give glory to Him;"
> **Revelation 19:6-7**

> "Praise, you servants of the Lord, praise the name of the Lord.
> ... From the rising and setting of the sun
> is the name of the Lord to be praised!
> High above all nations is the Lord; above the heavens is His glory!"
> **Psalm 113:1-4**

The Holy Bible tells us that the first to pay homage to Christ were some poor shepherds who were told by the angels to go to see the child. Back in those days, shepherds were disregarded people. They were considered to be very low in society, and not much attention was paid to these people. They were poor and rough around the edges. They were nobodies. It is interesting that the angels found these shepherds and appeared to them specifically, bringing them good news and inviting them to go and see for themselves, the Promised One. This shows how God has a special place in His heart for the downtrodden.

> And there were ... shepherds keeping watch over their flock by night.
> And behold an angel of the Lord stood by them and
> the glory of God shone round about them ... And the angel said to them,
> "Do not be afraid, for behold I bring you good news of great joy ...
> for today in the town of David a Saviour has been born to you,
> who is Christ the Lord."
>
> And suddenly there was with the angel
> a multitude of the heavenly host praising God and saying,
> "Glory to God in the highest, and on earth peace among men of good will!"
> ... And they came with haste: and they found Mary and Joseph,
> and the infant lying in the manger.
> **St. Luke 2:8-16**

Joseph rose from where he lay as he heard sounds from outside as though people were creeping about, and he feared that they might be thieves or troublemakers. The sounds crept closer and closer, and he could now hear people talking. Then the voices stopped until he heard a man's voice gently calling into the cave. The shepherds did not want to frighten anyone and feared their rough appearances might betray their good intentions, so they tried to sound more appeasing. Joseph, a little nervous, went to the opening to see who was calling on them at this hour. When he met them, he sighed with relief and knew they were good. Though they would have appeared gruff and a little intimidating, Joseph would have seen the gentleness and humility in their eyes. He would have seen in the shepherds his fellow workers, his neighbours, and his brothers. He felt love for them and warmly invited them in. Joseph and Mary, though tired, were glad to have visitors and the fact that they were shepherds made no difference to them. These men were in need of friends and so were the Holy Family.

> A kind mouth multiplies friends,
> and gracious lips prompt friendly greetings.
> ... A faithful friend is a sturdy shelter;
> he who finds one finds a treasure.
> A faithful friend is beyond price,
> no sum can balance his worth.
> **Sirach 6:5, 14-16**

The shepherds were invited to gaze upon the newborn, and they quietly approached the stone manger where He lay. How small and fragile was the Son of God, lying there in sweet repose. This royal child was not wrapped in sparkling clean Egyptian silk or velvet robes, but in humble swaddling clothes and Joseph's coat. Still the shepherds adored this child who would one day be known as the Good Shepherd and take His place as King of Heaven and Earth. We picture Mary and Joseph sharing what little they had with these men and conversing with them about the many things concerning the birth of their Son. They marvelled at what the shepherds told them about the multitude of angels and what they were told about their Son. We imagine this little gathering in the cave exchanging their angel stories through the night as Jesus slept in his humble crib. Mary would speak of the visit she had from the archangel Gabriel and how nervous but joyful she was at this encounter! How incredible that she would be hailed as being "full of grace"! Joseph would relate his angelic visit and how thankful he was for having received such a messenger, for it brought him back to his beloved, Mary! The shepherds would treasure this meeting with the Holy Family and Mary and Joseph would feel the same about the time they had spent with the shepherds!

> Mary kept all these words, pondering them in her heart.
> And the shepherds returned, glorifying and praising God
> for all the things they had heard and seen ...
> **St. Luke 2:19-20**

According to the apocryphal Arabic Infancy Gospel, the shepherds were not the only guests that night; another visitor was present even before the shepherds had arrived and was witness to the holiness of the Divine Infant Jesus:

> After sunset, the old woman [sick with Palsy] and Joseph with her,
> came to the cave, and they both went in.
> And, behold, it was filled with lights more beautiful
> than the gleaming of lamps and candles,
> and more splendid than the light of the sun.
> The child enwrapped in swaddling clothes,
> was sucking the breast of the lady Mary, His mother ...
>
> ... the old woman asked the lady Mary:
> "Art thou the mother of this child? ...
> Thou art not at all like the daughters of Eve."
> Mary replied: "... my son has no equal among children ...
> Place thy hands upon the child."
> And the old woman did so, and was immediately cured.
> **Arabic Infancy Gospel 3**

After all was said and done, the Holy Couple prepared to turn in for the night and get some much needed rest. Mary slept closest to their Son, with a smile on her face. Joseph gazed upon mother and child and noticed their eyes twitch ever so slightly. What dreams are they having? What thoughts are floating in the minds of his beautiful wife and child? Joseph also smiled and wondered if they were sharing their dreams with one another. As Joseph pondered this, his thoughts turned to prayer as he himself drifted to sleep.

> "O Lord, let the light of Your countenance shine upon us!
> You put gladness into my heart,
> more than when grain and wine abound.
> As soon as I lie down, I fall peacefully asleep,
> for You alone, O Lord, bring security to my dwelling."
> **Psalm 4:7-9**

The Carpenter's Son
Chapter 8: All in the Family

> We will declare to the generation to come the glorious deeds of the Lord
> and His strength and the wonders that He wrought...
> He commanded our fathers they should make known to their sons ...
> that they should put their hope in God ...
> **Psalm78:4-8**

Soon after our Lord was born, Joseph set out to register his family in the census. He most likely ran into his family and friends, who were also registering, and joyfully announced to them that he had just become a father! His heart on fire with love prompted him to tell them all that had taken place in the cave and the circumstances surrounding his son's birth. He told them about the shepherds' visit and how they paid homage to his wife and child. His relatives marvelled at hearing all this and congratulated him, wanting to pay homage as well.

Once Joseph had found a more suitable place to reside during their stay in Bethlehem, he went to the cave that housed Our Lord and Our Lady. He walked in quietly, so as not to disturb his newborn son and saw Mary rocking the child in her arms. They were bathed in light and as he approached, he felt as though he was in the presence of the Holy of Holies, which in reality he was. Jesus was being rocked back and forth as his humble mother softly sang this Jewish lullaby:

> "Maiden, maiden can I ask you,
> What can grow, grow without rain?
> What can burn, burn and not stop?
> What can cry, cry without tears?
>
> Foolish young man, what are you asking?
> A stone can grow, grow without rain,
> Love can burn, burn and not stop,
> A heart can cry, cry without tears."
> **Traditional Jewish Lullaby**

After her song, Mary looked up and smiled at Joseph, then gazed adoringly back at the infant. Joseph hadn't heard this song since he himself was a boy. So peaceful, so tranquil, the animals keep a quiet vigil for the mother and child. Joseph, lost in the beauty of this sight, crouched down next to them. He gazed at Jesus and saw him looking directly into his eyes, his little fingers wrapped around Joseph's thumb. Our Lady smiled and told him, "He's been waiting for you all morning." Joseph suddenly remembered what he had been in such a hurry to tell Mary. He excitedly told her the news that he'd found a better place for them to stay; he also told her how the registration went and about the family members he ran into while in town. Mary's eyes lit up, and she was happy with all he told her. Later that evening, a knock on the door and the cave was full of people. Mary was introduced to Joseph's relatives and they to her and their new baby brother. Why do I say baby "brother"? The Holy Bible asserts that Mary was a virgin both before and after she gave birth to Christ, which was discussed in Chapter 3. So who are these "brothers" of the Lord mentioned in the Gospel of St. Matthew and in the Acts of the Apostles?[5]

> While He was still speaking to the crowds,
> His mother and His *brothers* appeared outside,
> wishing to speak with Him.
> **St. Matthew 12:46**

> All these devoted themselves with one accord to prayer,
> together with some women and Mary the mother of Jesus, and His *brothers*.
> **Acts 1:14**

The expression "brothers and sisters" refers not only to actual siblings, but to first cousins and close relations. In Aramaic and Hebrew there was no word for "cousin," so "brother" or "sister" was used, which were general terms. This is the plain and simple truth. In the Bible, the word "brother" is used 350 times and the majority of these instances are *not* referring to an actual brother, as in the examples listed below.

> Tobiah went to look for someone acquainted with the roads
> who would travel with him to Media. As soon as he went out, he found
> the angel Raphael standing before him, though he did not know that he was
> an angel of God.
> Tobiah said to him, "Who are you, young man?" He replied

> "I am an Israelite, one of your *kinsmen*. I have come here to work.
> **Tobit 5:4-5**

> Raphael said to the boy: "*Brother* Tobiah!
> ... Tonight we must stay with your relative Raguel."
> **Tobit 6:11**

> Do not be surprised, *brethren*, if the world hates you.
> We know that we have passed from death to life,
> because we love the brethren.
> He who does not abide in love, abides in death.
> **1 St. John 3:13-15**

So, we go back to Joseph's family. According to early Church tradition, Joseph had a brother named Alpheus of Clophas who was wed to the Virgin Mary's sister, also named Mary. This Mary was the mother of James, Joses, Judas, and Simon who are all referred to as the brothers of Jesus.

> Standing by the cross of Jesus were
> His mother and His mother's sister, Mary the wife of Clopas...
> **St. John 19:25**

> Is this not the carpenter, the son of Mary,
> and the *brother* of James and Joses and Judas and Simon?
> **St. Mark 6:3**

Stating that Joseph had children with a previous wife or that Mary was not a virgin is *false*, and to say otherwise is to disbelieve the earliest Church Fathers and the Holy Bible. It is evident that Mary had no other children because while her only Son was hanging on the cross, bruised and bleeding, he felt compelled to entrust her into the care of his beloved Apostle, John. Joseph died before Christ entered into public ministry, so it would be up to his children to take her in. Why would Jesus give His mother to John if He had brothers or sisters to take care of her? Why were his brothers and sisters not at the foot of the cross with their mother? Are we to believe that these sons and daughters refused their mother? It doesn't make sense. So, feeling responsible for His mother's well-being, Christ gave her to His best friend to watch over. Even in the excruciating pain of His crucifixion, He cared enough to look after His mother till the very end.

> When Jesus therefore, saw His mother
> and the disciple standing by, whom He loved,
> He said to His mother, "Woman, behold thy son."
> Then He said to the disciple, "Behold thy mother."
> And from that hour the disciple took her into his home.
> ... And bowing His head, He gave up His spirit.
> **St. John 19:26-30**

One might argue that this example is not enough to suggest that Jesus was Mary's only child. To be crucified was the most shameful way to die, and perhaps this is why Jesus' so-called brothers were not at the foot of the cross with their mother. We can take note that not even His apostles were present, except of course for John the Beloved. Where were His apostles and friends? They might have been ashamed to be associated with the crucifixion –scene—as would His brothers. Still, if Jesus had brothers or sisters, He would not have needed to give His mother into the care of His friend, regardless of whether or not they were at the foot of the cross. Why would His brothers abandon not only Him, but their mother as well? If we take "brother" references literally, then out of four brothers, would not one of them support their mother? Would all four abandon her? Not likely.

Another example that could support the only-child story is shown to us in the Gospel of St. Luke. In this Gospel, we are told about an event in the late childhood of Jesus:

> And His parents were wont to go every year to Jerusalem
> at the Feast of the Passover.
> And when He was twelve years old, they went up to Jerusalem according to the custom of the feast. And after they had fulfilled the days, when they were returning, the boy Jesus remained in Jerusalem, and His parents did not know it. ... And it came to pass that after three days, that they found Him in the temple ...
> **St. Luke 2:41-47**

In this account, Jesus is almost a man in the eyes of the law, for thirteen is the age at which a Jewish boy reaches manhood. Joseph and Mary had now been husband and wife for twelve years, and yet Jesus is their only child mentioned. Surely if they had not made a vow of chastity, they would have had other children besides Jesus by then. The "brothers and sisters" of Christ would have been mentioned by now, and when would be more appropriate to mention them, than at a family pilgrimage to Jerusalem? Their extended family is mentioned, but no reference is made to "brothers" or "sisters" here. The Bible would have stated that "the boy Jesus was not among His brothers and sisters, nor among His relatives," but does not.

> ... it occurred to them to look for Him
> among their relatives and acquaintances.
> And not finding Him, they returned to Jerusalem in search of Him.
> ... they found Him in the temple, sitting in the midst of the teachers,
> listening to them and asking them questions ... And His mother said to Him,
> "Son, why hast thou done so to us? Behold, in sorrow thy father and I have
> been seeking Thee... And He went down with them to Nazareth,
> and was subject to them;
> And His mother kept all these things carefully in her heart.
> And Jesus advanced
> in wisdom and age and grace before God and men.
> **St. Luke 2:44-51**

Francisco Rizi, The Dream of St. Joseph, 1665, Spain

Raphael Sanzio of Urbino, The Holy Espousals, 1504, Italy

Ortolano, The Nativity with Saints, ca.1520, Italy

Leonardo Flores Workshop, Adoration of the Child Jesus, 1690, Bolivia

Unknown Artist, The Nativity (detail), 1660, Russia

Fernando de los Santos, The Return From Egypt, 1507, Spain

Bartolome Esteban Murillo, St. Joseph and the Holy Child, ca.1665, Spain

Bartolome Esteban Murillo, The Two Trinities, 1681, Spain

El Greco, St. Joseph Leading the Child Jesus, 1598, Spain

Unknown Artist, Heaven and Earth Trinities, 18th Century, Peru

Juan del Castillo, The Death of St. Joseph, 1630, Spain

Joseph de Ybarra, The Coronation of Joseph (detail), 1735, Mexico

Unknown Artist, Photo by Author, St. Joseph and the Child Jesus, Portugal

Juan Sanchez Cotan, St. Joseph Leading the Christ Child, ca.1610, Spain

The Carpenter's Son
Chapter 9: First Drops of Blood

> "Every male among you shall be circumcised.
> ... it shall be a token of the covenant between you and Me."
> **Genesis 17:10-12**

Eight days after the birth of a son, the Law required him to be circumcised. This rite was prescribed by God to Abraham as a sign of His close union with His people. The circumcision of a son was not just a "procedure" back then, but a solemn and joyful occasion! Word would be sent to friends and relatives to join them in the celebration and just as we celebrate the Baptism of a child, so too did they celebrate the circumcision! This meaningful ceremony was fulfilling the Jews' part of their covenant with God. This sacred rite was so family oriented that it didn't even have to take place at the temple. In fact, they didn't even need a priest, it could be done by the father, mother, brother, –neighbour—anyone! In the Bible, we are given examples of males being circumcised without the need for a priest:

> ... Sepphora took a piece of flint
> and cut off her son's foreskin and, touching his feet she said,
> ... "You are a spouse of blood," in regard to the circumcision.
> **Exodus 4:25-27**

> And behold, a certain disciple named Timothy,
> son of a believing Jewess, but of a Gentile father.
> ... This man, Paul wished to go forth with him, and he took and
> circumcised him on account of the Jews who were in those parts ...
> **Acts 16:1-4**

So who carried out the Holy Child's circumcision? His chosen father, Joseph. He would have the honour of performing this rite on his son and bestowing upon Him the name of Jesus, the angel's voice sounding clear in his mind: "You will call him Jesus."

As Joseph performed the circumcision, his heart was heavy as he heard the cries of his son and saw the first drops of blood. But soon after, his heart was filled with joy as he announced the child's name: "His name is Jesus!" Since the beginning of time Joseph was chosen, just as Mary was, to play an important role in the history of mankind. Joseph was the first man to utter the name of our Saviour. His lips were the first to pronounce the Holy Name of Jesus. How the heavens must have rejoiced at this moment as the name of Salvation was spoken!

It is very important that the Bible notes the circumcision of the Infant Jesus not only by reminding us of God's presence with His people, but also to prove the reality of His human nature against those who do not believe that Jesus was God-made-flesh. Jesus is *both* human and divine, but there were some who believed that Jesus was not human at all, but only divine and in the illusion of a body. They did not believe that he took on a human body that had been formed for nine months in the womb of the Virgin Mary! If baby Jesus didn't have a human body, then who did Joseph circumcise!?

If you deny the human aspect of Jesus, you are denying that He was able to suffer and die for the salvation of mankind.

In most Russian icons, Jesus is depicted as holding up His right hand and giving us the "peace" sign. He holds up his index and middle finger side –by side and folds in His thumb and remaining fingers. In these pictures, Jesus appears to be blessing the viewer, but there is also a deeper meaning to the arrangement of his fingers. For the longest time, I didn't know what it was, but one day my priest explained to me the true meaning: The two raised fingers symbolize His two natures: He is both God and Man. The three folded fingers symbolize the Holy Trinity: the Father, Son, and Holy Spirit. The circumcision proves to us that God literally took on human flesh, while still retaining His divinity. And Joseph gives us the proof that Jesus was indeed flesh and blood. God became one of us. So simple!

And when eight days were fulfilled for His circumcision,
His name was called Jesus, the name given Him by the angel
before He was conceived in the womb.
St. Luke 2:21

And the Word was made flesh, and dwelt among us.
And we saw His –glory—glory as of the only-begotten of the Father
—full of grace and of truth.
St. John 1:14

The Carpenter's Son
Chapter 10: The Ransom

> "When a woman has conceived and gives birth
> to a boy ... she shall spend thirty-three days more
> in becoming purified of her blood ..."
> **Leviticus 12:2, 4**

After the circumcision, Joseph found work to support his family during their stay in Bethlehem. It was his plan that his family should live there until after the purification in the temple. Joseph would set up a small shop and do carpentry for the town's residents. Thirty-three days after Our Lord's circumcision, it was time for Joseph to take his wife and son to the temple at Jerusalem. The Law stated that after the birth of a child, the mother had to be purified, and though Mary herself was pure in her virginity, she was still subject to the Law in those days, as was Jesus. Joseph would have to make two offerings: one for his wife to be purified and one as ransom for his son. The presentation was a ceremony in which the father would "buy back" his son from God. Under Jewish Law, the first-born son was reserved especially for God, and so was "presented" to Him. The child would then be "bought back" with an offering to the Lord. Joseph and Mary sought to follow the Law as perfectly as possible and had a deep respect for it.

> When the days of her purification were fulfilled
> according to the Law of Moses, they took him up
> to Jerusalem to present him to the Lord ...
> **St. Luke 2:22**

After leaving Bethlehem early in the morning, the Holy Family arrived at the temple. Such awe and reverence would they have felt upon seeing the mighty temple! So many people going in and coming out, but one particular person stood out. Joseph noticed a suspicious old man watching him and his wife, though he did not tell Mary. He had heard stories of strange people in Jerusalem, and so he trusted no one. As they got closer to the temple, Joseph's suspicions faded as he was awestruck by the beautiful temple and its surroundings. The temple was divided into different places: one area reserved for men only and another for women. There would have been other families there as well undergoing the purification and presentation. Mary would have been a bit nervous as she had never done this before. Joseph reassured her and instructed her on what to do. He reached into one of his bundles ,took out a few coins, and handed them to Mary. He pointed to the women's gate and told her what she had to do. Joseph took his son in his arms and seemed to fumble as he carefully tried to hold the infant properly. He was scared he might drop him as he arranged the –child—he was still not used to holding a –baby—and was over careful while holding him. Watching this man fumble with his baby boy made Mary laugh! She told him to relax a little and that holding a baby is not complicated. She smiled as she showed him the simple but proper way. Mary went over to the women's gate and dropped the coin offerings into one of the large clay jars. Then she prayed, as the other women were doing, until a horn sounded. That was the signal that the women were to approach and proceed up the fifteen steps to the Nicanor Gate.

There, more prayers were said and incense was burned for the women. Blue clouds of perfumed smoke rose to the morning sky as the women were purified and they rejoiced!

> "Behold I come; in the written scroll
> it is prescribed for me, to do Your will, O my God,
> is my delight, and Your law is within my heart!"
> **Psalm 40:8-10**

After Mary was finished, she returned to her husband and son who were waiting outside. She looked down at Jesus and saw that He was looking intently at his father. His eyes then turned to His mother's, and so Joseph handed the child to her. It was now time for him to do his part at the temple. Joseph walked to a corner stand in the outer temple's marketplace and asked the merchant, "May I please have two turtledoves, for my son is about to be presented and ransomed." The man behind the counter gave him the two turtledoves in a cage, and Joseph paid him. As he made his way to the temple, he looked back at his family and saw Mary sitting and rocking her son as she sang to him. Even at the busy temple, Mary and Jesus were in their own quiet world. The serenity of the moment was broken when suddenly Joseph saw the strange old man who had been watching them earlier, now rushing towards them!

Joseph ran and called to his wife to watch out, but just as quickly as the old man was rushing to Mary, so too did he stop just short of a few feet in front of them. Joseph dashed in front of him and shielded his wife and son, angrily demanding to know what was going on. "What are you doing approaching my wife like a madman? Why have you been watching us? What is your business with us?" The old man looked scared and started to stammer as a temple official stepped in. Joseph told him what had happened, and the guard smiled and explained who the old man was. "Forgive him, for he is always at our temple seeking the Messiah." Joseph gave the guard and the old man a confused look. The soldier put his arm around the old man and said, "Do not be afraid of him. His name is Simeon, and he is a devout man. You see, he claims to be filled with the Holy Spirit and was told that he would not leave this earth until he has seen the Saviour who was promised to us. He comes to the temple every day to meet every child who is presented here, in the hopes that one of these will be the Promised One." Simeon looked at Joseph and then looked towards Mary and humbly apologized for scaring them. He timidly asked if he could hold the child for just a moment. Mary looked at the guard and then at Joseph, who sighed and nodded his approval. Simeon delicately held the child. He looked down and smiled, and soon tears were rolling down his cheeks. His glistening eyes looked up at the parents, and he said to them: "It is Him!" He then looked up towards Heaven and blessed God, saying:

"Now thou dost dismiss Thy servant, O Lord,
according to Thy word, in peace;
because my eyes have seen Thy salvation,
which Thou hast prepared before the face of all peoples:
a light of revelation to the Gentiles, and a glory for Thy people Israel!"
And [Joseph and Mary] were marvelling
at the things spoken concerning him.
St. Luke 2:29-3

Just as the shepherds had told them things concerning their Son, so too had Simeon. Joseph and Mary pondered these things, wondering what exactly this man had just told them. Their Son would become a great wonder to people, but how exactly would this be so?

It was now time to pay the ransom for their Son. Joseph walked towards the temple again, and a priest approached him, "What is your business with the temple today?"

Joseph replied, "My business is to redeem my Son, to purchase Him back for me." The priest then said, "In the Law of the Lord it is written that you shall sacrifice a yearling lamb and a pigeon." Joseph looked uneasy and started to tell the priest that he could not afford to buy a lamb. He held up his cage of turtledoves. This was known as the "offering of the poor." The priest then said not to worry, that they were also acceptable.

... as it is written in the Law of the Lord,
Every male child that opens the womb shall be called holy to the Lord
- and to offer a sacrifice ... "a pair of turtledoves or two young pigeons."
St. Luke 2:23-25

The Lord spoke to Moses and said,
"Consecrate to Me every firstborn that opens the womb...
for it belongs to me."
Exodus 13:1-2

The priest took the cage and escorted Joseph to a side altar. This side altar was special and used for sacrifices to the Lord. Joseph stopped at the bottom of the steps, looked up, and saw flames coming from the top. The priest turned around and beckoned him to follow him to the top, which is where the ceremony took place. Once they reached the top, Joseph saw the pit of fire and felt the heat emanating. He pulled out one of the turtledoves and handed it over to the priest who showed him what to do with it. The priest took a knife and showed how Joseph was to kill the bird, and he said, "Now, my son, it is your turn." Joseph then took the first dove, slit its throat, and handed it to the priest. The priest took it and sprinkled the blood on the altar and then it into the firepit. Joseph repeated this with the second dove as did the priest. After they had finished, Joseph felt something different within him. His face was now serene and radiant with a bright smile upon it. The priest was talking to him, but he couldn't hear him as he was totally immersed in God.

The priest said, "Well, my son, I shall leave you with your thoughts,", and walked down the steps. After some time, Joseph returned to his senses. He prayed for a little while then remembered that his wife and child were still waiting for him! So, he rushed out of the temple to meet them.

There are some people who believe that after the ceremony was finished, Joseph was in an ecstasy and beheld St. Gabriel the Archangel, who once again had a message for him. The message below is given to us from a visionary in the United States who has reportedly received messages and visions from the Holy Family. As these visions have, as of yet, not ceased, the Church has made no judgment either supporting or opposing these reported apparitions. The message from Gabriel to Joseph, as related below, is given to us by the – visionary—who is submissive to the Church's ultimate judgment.

"Now Son of David, Joseph,
you have redeemed and purchased this holy child as your own.
Protect Him, care for Him, and watch over Him for the rest of your days,
for His sorrows shall be your sorrows and His joys your joys!
And also the holy mother, she too shall bear the seed of joy
and sorrow and peace for you.
You shall ever be known as the head of the family.
Guard carefully the spouse and the child entrusted to you.
You have purchased this child as your own son.

Accept Him as your own son and bring Him up in the way of the Lord.
And behold this message I give to you, for you shall not live long
after the boy turns twenty.
He is the Son of God, the living Messiah, and he shall
save the people from their sins.
You have prayed for this and so has His mother.
Now He is here and is appointed by God to be the living sacrifice
and to reconcile this people to their Father."

Related by Chris Courtis, Visionary, in Maryland, U.S.A.
September 13, 2005

As the Holy Family started on their journey back to Bethlehem, Joseph contemplated what Simeon had said about his Son. Jesus was called "Israel's Salvation," but how would He be their salvation? So far, he had been told nothing but incredible things concerning his Son: the Child was only forty days old and already He was given the responsibility of "Saving Israel"! How would this child, a carpenter's son, do this? But, from all those who spoke of his Son, there was the consistent theme of the Child's greatness! First, the words of his beloved Mary, relating the words of the angel: "He will be great, and will be called the Son of the Most High!" After the visitation, Mary told Joseph the words of her cousin Elizabeth: "Blessed is the fruit of thy womb!" Next, the angel Gabriel himself told Joseph: "He shall save His people from their sins!" Following this we have the testimony of the shepherds, Simeon, and the prophetess Anna, who had seen the child at the temple, and began then to praise the Lord:

> "A Saviour has been born! Justice shall be his waistband and faithfulness a belt upon his hips! And He shall be the glory of Israel and the salvation of all people!"

Joseph also recalled the second part of Simeon's message, and tried to understand what it all meant. Simeon's message is bittersweet as it is full of joy and hope, but also isolation and sadness:

> And Simeon blessed them, and said to Mary his mother, "Behold, this child is destined for the fall and rise of many ... ... And thy own soul a sword shall pierce, that the thoughts of many hearts may be revealed."
> **St. Luke 2:28-35**

The air of calm surrounding Jesus was now giving way to a dark cloud. Yes, their Son would be a great man—a light to the world—and yet one day He would be rejected and His mother's heart would suffer in union with His. What was Mary to think of this? Her Son was not even two months old and already such things were being said about Him. How heavy her heart must have been at hearing these words. She looked at Joseph and saw that he was distraught. He wondered why and how his Son would face such things and Mary as well. There was no mention of Joseph in the prophecy, and he must have assumed that meant he would not be alive to protect his family this time. How would a husband feel knowing that his wife and son were to suffer, and there wasn't a thing he could do about it? He would feel deep sorrow, panic, and helplessness. But thus far, God had not let them down, so he would have had to trust that everything would be as God wanted. Mary's very soul would be pierced along with her Son's, and this would be realized years later as she watched in horror as her Son was whipped, beaten, and spat upon, but the worst was to come. She would be at the foot of the cross to which her only Son was nailed. What mother wouldn't want to kiss her son's bruises and alleviate his pain? Her heart would be wounded with grief beyond measure, and her husband would not be there for her to lean on. Joseph would try to understand Simeon's prophecy and what it meant to his Son and wife and why Joseph himself would not be there to comfort either. Though their hearts were heavy, they must live their lives and carry on.

Joseph and Mary were told that many would fall and many would rise on account of their Son, but how could Jesus be the fall of anyone? God sent Jesus to this world for the salvation of mankind, not for our downfall and not to condemn us. Man has free will, and therefore he chooses to fall. Jesus was sent to hold out His hand to others, not to point the finger. Mary was told that she would be involved in her Son's –mission—whatever it might –be—and her very soul would be an instrument for others to use, as the inner thoughts of people would be shown through this. How would the piercing of Mary's heart allow for others' thoughts to be revealed? And how would this come about? It would not come about until years later, after Joseph's death, and the beginning of her Son's ministry. Joseph could not comprehend at this time and was not yet meant to know. Though Joseph did not understand everything, he was nonetheless amazed at hearing everything that Simeon had told them, and he too treasured all of these things in his chaste, paternal heart. His Son and wife were special to –him—they meant more to him than his own –life— but one day they would be special to the entire world!

O Lord, our Lord, how glorious is Your name all over the earth!
... Out of the mouth of babes and sucklings You have fashioned praise!
What is ... the Son of Man that You should care for him?
You have made him little less than the angels,
and crowned him with glory and honour!
Psalm 8:1-5

The Carpenter's Son
Chapter 11: The Child Hunted

"Arise, and take the child and his mother,
and flee into Egypt, and remain there until I tell thee!
For Herod will seek the child to destroy him!"
St. Matthew 2:13

Joseph woke up suddenly, his heart pounding quickly and heavily, his body covered in sweat. He had to get his family out of Bethlehem as soon as possible! The angel who had appeared to him before had come back again tonight with an alarming and terrifying message: King Herod wanted their son dead! Herod was a tyrannical ruler who was notorious for his foul temper. Everyone knew of him, but they knew even more of the crimes and scandals associated with him. He treated his people in such a cruel –way—even his family was not exempt from his cruelty: he had murdered his wife and three of his sons! His own flesh and blood! Joseph didn't know why Herod wanted to kill the child Jesus, nor did he have time to think about this, all he knew was he had to get his Son to safety. He woke Mary and tried to calmly tell her that they had to leave right away. She was coming out of sleep and wasn't sure what was going on as Joseph frantically scurried around the house packing up their belongings. "Mary, hurry, we have to leave, right now! We have to hide!"

"Hide ... from what? What is going on?" she asked. "The angel came to me again, and he told me that Herod seeks to kill our Son! We must flee to Egypt and await further instruction!"

Mary got up and quickly wrapped her baby in extra blankets. She threw on an extra shawl, and by now Joseph had the donkey all ready to go. They quietly stole away into the night, moving like shadows in the street.

The night would have been cold and dark, their only lamp the light of the moon and the stars in the sky. As Joseph guided the donkey out of Bethlehem, he pondered in his heart: "Why would a king want to hurt an innocent child? What has my son done to warrant this murderous plot? He's just a baby!" Mary, too, wondered with Joseph as to why this child was a target for Herod's anger. The words of Simeon, the old man from the temple, echoed in their minds: "Behold, this child is destined for the fall and rise of many!" Could this already be the beginning fulfillment of his words? Jesus was barely two months old and already he had stirred up hope in the lowly and fear in the mighty! "Perhaps Herod believes our son to be a threat to him. But how?"

It turned out that King Herod was seeking the child who was foretold to be the "King of the Jews." As Herod was king, he was afraid that this child would grow up to take away his crown. Herod was told by wise men from the East, who knew everything concerning the prophecies of this future king and Messiah, that this child has already been born, and that He was in Bethlehem. Hearing this, he sent the wise men to Bethlehem to find the child and upon returning to tell him exactly where in Bethlehem this future ruler was, so that he too might pay homage to the infant king. Herod was using these men for his own evil purposes. When they found Jesus, they worshipped Him and rejoiced! They knew that Jesus was very special and that He was the Promised Redeemer! After the wise men found and visited the Holy Family, and angel appeared to them telling them of Herod's true intentions.

They felt terrible for they had almost led Herod to the child! They listened to the angel and went back home, avoiding Herod.

> ... and falling down they worshipped Him.
> And opening their treasures they offered Him gifts
> of gold, frankincense, and myrrh. And being warned in a dream
> not to return to Herod, they went back to their own country by another way.
> **St. Matthew 2:11-13**

Herod was furious at being deceived by the wise men and unleashed his anger by sending his soldiers to Bethlehem to kill every boy under the age of two, just to be sure. While soldiers were swarming into Bethlehem and tearing infants away from their mothers' breasts, Mary and Joseph were already far into the desert. Mary knew what was happening, and tears rolled down her face and dripped off her chin as she contemplated this savage killing of innocent children. She looked down at the child Jesus: "My poor son, we mustn't worry, for your father is a good man. He will take care of us and God will be our guide." The baby was asleep as His mother reassured Him, but in actuality she was also reassuring herself. Surely her heart was breaking. The sun was now beginning to rise, and their cover of darkness was slowly vanishing. She prayed silently over her boy, her lips whispering a prayer for divine help in her hour of need and especially for Joseph, her just husband:

> "Hearken to my words, O Lord,
> attend to my sighing. Heed my call for help, my king and my God!
> To You I pray, O Lord; at dawn You hear my voice;
> at dawn I bring my plea expectantly before you.
> Protect [us], that You may be the joy of [us] who love Your name!
> ... O Lord, bless the just man ...
> surround him with the shield of Your good will."
> **Psalm 5:2-5, 12**

Though his wife was praying quietly, Joseph heard her pleas to the Lord and was touched by her total confidence and faith in God. She was a strong woman and though she cried, her tears filled him with the strength to walk onwards, regardless of how tired his feet were.

> Thus says the Lord: "Cease your cries of mourning,
> wipe the tears from your eyes.
> The sorrow you have shown shall have its reward ..."
> **Jeremiah 31:16**

Christ was his love and salvation, and though He was not flesh of his flesh or blood of his blood, He was still his son! And as long as he kept his faith in the –Lord—especially during trials and –sufferings—Joseph would not fail! As the terrain turned rougher, the family spent several days walking in the hot sun and sleeping out in the open with no shelter above their heads. Also, Joseph got very little sleep since he kept watch almost all night. He had heard stories of people being robbed, raped, even killed in the desert! There is even a tradition in the Coptic Church that the Holy Family themselves encountered thieves in the desert:

> ... and turning away from this place, they came to a desert;
> and hearing that it was infested by robbers, Joseph and Mary
> resolved to cross this region by night. But as they went along, behold
> they saw two robbers lying in the way ...
> These two robbers were Titus and Dumachus.
> ... Titus said, "Let these persons go freely" and Dumachus refused.
> Titus said, "Take forty coins from me and hold this as a pledge"...
> And Mary, seeing that he had done this kindness said to him
> "The Lord will sustain thee for thy kindness."
> **Arabic Infancy Gospel 23**

The desert was no man's land save for thieves and snakes. On the rare occasions that they encountered a group of nomads, Joseph would cautiously approach –them—after hiding his wife and –child—to see if they had good intentions and if they had any food to spare, as their supplies were running low. He would accept only what was offered and would decipher if this group was noble or not to be trusted. If they were in fact well-meaning people, he would bring Mary and Jesus along to eat and rest. These encounters were few, but we imagine that they must have run into *some* people, as there would be other cautious travellers going to or from Egypt. But these rest stops were few and lasted only a few moments as they were not safe until they reached Egypt.

Meanwhile, Herod's fury raged in Bethlehem and its surrounding towns, innocent blood streamed down the streets as mothers and fathers wept for their sons. Joseph saw his wife's tears as she thought about these –families— families that were just like theirs. Joseph, though strong on the outside, was weeping bitterly in his heart. Just thinking about the fathers wrestling to save their sons made his heart swell with sorrow. Had the angel not warned him, it would have been *him*, fighting to save his only Son! It would have been *his wife*, sobbing in the streets! It would have been *his boy* who was killed by the sword of a jealous king! These men's sons would be the first martyrs to spill their blood for Jesus Christ. These Holy Innocents died for Christ without even knowing it, but great is their reward in Heaven.

... and he sent and slew all the boys
in Bethlehem and all its neighbourhood
who were two years old or under ...
St. Matthew 2:16

In Ramah is heard the sound of moaning, of bitter weeping!
Rachel mourns her children, she refuses to be consoled because her children
are no more...
Jeremiah 31:15

... I saw under the altar, the souls
of those who had been slain for the Word of God,
... and they cried out with a loud voice, saying,
"How long, O Lord, (holy and true), dost Thou refrain from
judging and from avenging our blood on those who dwell on the earth?"
Revelation 6:9

The Carpenter's Son
Chapter 12: An Egyptian Home

> So he arose and took the child and his mother
> by night, and withdrew into Egypt.
> **St. Matthew 2:14**

After days of hazardous travel, Joseph finally saw the great pyramids against the backdrop of the orange, Egyptian sky. A sigh of relief would have escaped the lips of Mary and her husband. They were now safe, but as they made their way though Egypt, they received many strange looks from people as they were foreigners and were not to be trusted. Joseph would have had to repeat his actions in Bethlehem. Having to settle in another country, make a home, and find work was beginning to take its toll on Joseph. Everything had happened so quickly since marrying his beloved: first he had the dilemma of his virgin bride being found pregnant with the Son of God. He had stressed so much over this, and his heart was full of fear and anxiety until the angel had appeared to him and reassured him. Second, once he and Mary were husband and wife, he had to travel to Bethlehem for the census. This journey was hard for him, especially since Mary was already nearly ready to give birth, and having arrived there, having to find shelter as his wife was having contractions! Once he had found shelter in the cave, and Mary had given birth to our Lord, he had to sleep with one eye open. He was protective of his wife and child and would hear sounds at night, scared that thieves or other criminals might seek to hide there or worse, to rob them of the few possessions they had!

After this, Joseph had been told of King Herod's intentions to have the child executed, and he had to flee with Mary and Jesus in the middle of the night. He saw the children of Bethlehem in his mind, and he wept for them! He wept for his wife, whose heart was breaking at the thought of all those innocents being taken away from their own mothers! He wept for his Son, who was being persecuted by a man who had killed even *his* own sons! The steps to Egypt were stained with the tears of Joseph and Mary as they travelled the rough terrain under the hot sun and cold night sky. The child Jesus was carried into a foreign land as a fugitive, though He had committed no crime. They finally arrived in Egypt, not as tourists but as refugees running from their own country! Their refuge was in Egypt, the land of "gods and goddesses," so imagine how Joseph and Mary would have felt. They were faithful Jews who lived in the Law and worshipped the one God of Abraham, not Ra, Osiris, or the many other gods of the Egyptians! But little did the Egyptians know that in their midst was the One True God.

> See, the Lord is riding ... (into) Egypt;
> the idols of Egypt tremble before Him,
> the hearts of the Egyptians melt within them.
> **Isaiah 19:1**

It is believed that that Holy Family did not just settle at the first town or city they encountered, but were constantly on the move in order to find a suitable place of safety. The angel did not tell Joseph how long they would have to stay in exile, so until hearing again from the messenger, they would travel Egypt. Tradition states that they stayed in Egypt for three years before returning to their homeland and settling in Nazareth. According to Eastern tradition, Theophilus the Coptic Patriarch of Alexandria from A.D. 385-412, had a vision in which he was shown the Holy Family's escape route and the many places in Egypt at which they rested. He states that Joseph and his family fled from Bethlehem to Gaza, and then to El-Zaraniq, which is about thirty-eight kilometres west of El-Arish. From there they travelled along northern Sinai and stopped in Farma. After this they were safe, as they had left the harsh wilderness behind them. After weeks of further travel, they made plenty of rest stops, among them Matariyah. At this place a tree stands, very simply called "Mary's Tree." It was here that they rested in the tree's shade, and a miracle was performed by the Divine Infant. It is believed that Jesus caused water to flow from a spring, from which they all drank, and afterwards, the Virgin washed His clothes in this water. After washing His clothes, Mary poured the washing water onto the ground from which a sweet smelling balsam plant sprouted. It is there to this day and is said to have curative properties. No doubt that Joseph and Mary would be amazed by this. Whether this is true or not, the fact that the tradition carries on to this day is in itself a miracle. We are always seeking traces of the divine here on earth, and there is no reason why this tree could not be one that had the privilege of shading the Holy Family.
Another tradition, this one taken from the Pseudo-Gospel of Matthew, has inspired many artists in painting what is popularly known as "The Rest on the Flight into Egypt." This tradition also speaks of a tree and a miracle:

And it came to pass on the third day of their journey…
that the blessed Mary was fatigued by the excessive heat of the sun …
and seeing a palm tree, she said to Joseph:
"Let me rest a little under the shade of this tree."
Joseph therefore made haste, and led her to the palm …
And as the blessed Mary was sitting there,
she looked up to the foliage of the palm, and saw it full of fruit, and said to
Joseph: "I wish it were possible to get some of the fruit of this palm."
And Joseph said to her:
"I wonder that you say this, when you see how high the palm tree is."
Then the child Jesus … said to the palm:
"O tree, bend your branches, and refresh my mother with your fruit."
And immediately at these words the palm bent its top down
to the very feet of the blessed Mary; and they gathered from it fruit,
with which they were all refreshed.
The Gospel of Pseudo-Matthew

In this tradition, Mary is exhausted and wishes to rest a while in the shade of a tree. She does not want to trouble her husband—after all he has been doing most of the walking, and yet he does not seek rest until his bride recommends it. He is totally faithful to his spouse. When she mentions that she is tired and would like to rest, Joseph acts straightaway—just as he always has. He was given a request and he faithfully complied. This is not to portray Joseph as a pushover, but rather as a man who puts his family first in every way. Next, Mary tells him that she is hungry and would like some fruit. The only fruit available is at the top of a very tall date palm tree, and though he would gladly try to climb up there for her, he knows it would be difficult and basically tells her it's going to be a tough job getting way up there, and perhaps she didn't realize how high it really was? The child Jesus, quietly listening to His parents, decides to help them. It is as if Mary went to Joseph, and Joseph went to Jesus by way of his statement. In the end, Mary's request is granted by miraculous means and everybody is happy.

Eventually Joseph led his family to Mount Qussqam, which would be their home for the next few years. Now there is a great monastery and church there, its altar stone held to be the resting place of the child Jesus during this stay with His parents here. This new home would be the most meaningful of all their rests in Egypt because it was seen as yet another fulfillment of the Old Testament prophecy of Isaiah.

> On that day there shall be an altar to the Lord in the land of Egypt...
> **Isaiah 19:19**

Joseph would struggle at the beginning, but in the end he would have a home for his family and work to provide for them. He would either set up a small shop or join other shops or contractors. He would have been uneasy at first, since he did not know the language or the customs of the Egyptians, but he pulled through and made the best of his situation. There were Jewish communities in Egypt as well, such as in Ain Shams, so it is reasonable to say that Joseph would have found some workers who knew his language and customs, and they would have supported one another. He did not judge his neighbours who worshipped the many gods of the land, but he was steadfast in his own faith and led by example.

It must have been incredibly difficult to go into exile, especially for a young family who were just starting out. But we can see that every time Joseph is handed a trial or some serious problem, he doesn't sit and ask a million questions and then feel sorry for himself because he feels helpless. He listens to the angel's command and obeys. He would, of course, have wanted to have asked questions, but he recognized that since the orders were from God, he would not require anything else. No time for nonsense! He acts right away! The Holy Bible tells us this:

> So Joseph, arising from sleep,
> did as the angel of the Lord had commanded him...
> **St. Matthew 1:24**

He placed his trust in God and knew that He would provide for –him—even in the hardest of times when it seemed that the Lord had abandoned him. It is human to sometimes feel that God is no longer with us or that He has stopped listening to us because we feel the need for constant comfort and reassurance. We don't always get this warm feeling and we often feel like we are left in the cold to fend for ourselves. We assume that many refugees feel this way; those who are forced to run away and go into hiding are afraid. Do we doubt that Joseph ever felt this way? We shouldn't. Joseph, though especially chosen by God, was also a human being. He was not divine. He did not have special powers. He was a man. A man with human frailties and weaknesses, *but* he was a man of intense faith! He recognized his need for God's help and in doing so was elevated in his dignity as a man. Joseph knew that he had only to ask for the necessities of daily life. God knows that we worry when we shouldn't and that we are quick to feel lost and alone. The carpenter was humble, and every time his family faced hardships, then overcame them, he knew it was because of his God. We can fall a thousand times, but the harder we fall, the prouder He is of us for getting back up! Joseph was a true example of this! With God we can do anything! We have only to ask for His help.

The Lord was with (him) so that he was successful...
The Lord was with him and (he) prospered in all his undertakings.
Genesis 39:2-4

I rejoice in the Lord and exult in my saving God!
God, my Lord, is my strength; He makes my feet swift...
Habakkuk 3:18-19

The Carpenter's Son
Chapter 13: Hidden Fatherhood

> And they kept saying,
> "Is this not Jesus the son of Joseph?"
> **St. John 6:42**

Joseph and Mary would spend the next three years in Egypt with their only Son and would eventually get accustomed to their current refugee status and go about their day to day lives. Joseph no doubt thought about the life he had left behind in Israel. Would he ever see his friends and relations again? Did they even know where he and his family were? Probably not since he had been awakened suddenly at night to take the child and His mother and flee into a foreign land. He didn't have the chance to tell anyone. For all they knew, Jesus had been murdered by Herod's soldiers along with all the other boys his age. And as for Joseph and Mary, who knows? Perhaps they had decided to make their permanent home in Bethlehem, the town which cradled their Son's lifeless body. Though he didn't preoccupy himself with these thoughts, he still worried about his family and friends back home, however he knew that one day he would be among them and life would get back to normal—whatever normal was.[6]

It was reportedly at Al-Muharraq that the messenger angel came once again to instruct the Lord's most humble servant. Joseph had been waiting for this moment for quite some time and finally it came to him.

> Arise, and take the young child and His mother,
> and go into the land of Israel; for they are dead
> which sought the young child's life.
> **Matthew 2:20-21**

Such relief! Joseph's paternal heart was overjoyed that he could now bring his Son and wife home. Though King Herod was dead and his soldiers had stopped hunting for the child, there was still reason to be somewhat wary, for the new king might have the same ideas as his predecessor. But since the angel of the Lord himself advised Joseph to return home, he would faithfully obey and carry out God's command. Joseph's complete trust in God was what moved his feet across the many miles of rough terrain.

The entire journey from Bethlehem into Al-Muharraq and back to Nazareth had covered roughly two thousand kilometres. Joseph, the Just Man, who would have walked the entire way, leading his family into and out of exile, would have taken over 2,500,000 steps for the greater glory of God! Though the years of exile were built on the foundation of despair, the return home was built on joy. His faith continued to guide him forward.

> But the path of the just is like shining light that grows
> in brilliance till perfect day ...
> Let your eyes look straight ahead and your glance be directly forward.
> Survey the path for your feet, and let all your ways be sure.
> **Proverbs 4:19, 25-26**

> "In Joseph, faith is not separated from action. His faith had a decisive effect
> on his actions. Paradoxically, it was by acting,
> by carrying out his responsibilities,
> that he stepped aside and left God free to act,
> placing no obstacles in his way.
> Joseph is a 'just' man because his existence is 'ad-justed'
> to the word of God."
> **Pope Benedict XVI**
> *Yaoundé, Cameroon, March 18, 2009*

Had this exile been a test given by God, surely Joseph had not only passed it, but had raised the bar for fathers to come. The Heavenly Father has given us a completely human father as a blueprint for what true paternity is. Joseph is God's model of real fatherhood, Mary is our perfect image of motherhood, and Christ is our ideal of true and perfect brotherhood. Because of this earthly trinity, we have the perfect family blueprint for the most imperfect of times.

Joseph teaches us that fatherhood goes beyond genetics, and now more than ever he is a role model for both biological and adoptive parents. Though Christ is not flesh of his flesh, blood of his blood, he accepts the life that grows within the sanctuary of his beloved's womb. From the moment that Jesus was conceived by the power of the Holy Spirit, He took on the human nature of His chosen father, Joseph, and the flesh and blood of Our Lady. When he accepted the role of father, he became the Patron of the Unborn, the loving guardian of the helpless and innocent. Just as he loved the unborn Redeemer while still in His mother's womb, so too does he love all the unborn children of this world. And just as he wept for the children who were massacred by King Herod, so too does he now weep for those who are aborted in clinics, every day, all around the world.

> Behold, sons are a gift from the Lord;
> the fruit of the womb is a reward.
> **Psalms 126:3**

> Truly you have formed my inmost being;
> You knit me in my mother's womb.
> I give You thanks that I am fearfully, wonderfully made;
> wonderful are Your works. My soul also knew You full well;
> **Psalms 139:13-16**

Joseph is also a model for those men who are afraid or hesitant to take on the responsibility of raising a child. So many young men are faced with the news that their wife or girlfriend is pregnant. A flood of panic overtakes many of them, especially those who are unmarried, and in their despair they run away from their responsibilities, abandoning mother and child. It is this act of abandonment that that leads many children to be aborted by their mothers, not out of malice but out of worry and fear. Who better to be a guide for these men, than one who's been there? Joseph was faced with the exact same situation as these men and almost resorted to sending his beloved, and the Child within her, away! In the end though, he took his honourable place as husband and father. He knows what it was like to almost lose his wife and Son, and if men would only look to him, chosen by the Eternal Father, they would know that he understands how they feel. He really does. He felt confused, scared, and full of anxiety, but the love of a father for his son outweighs all of these frustrations. He was truly predestined above all other men to take on the role of Father of the Redeemer.

The Holy Bible does not give us an account of the childhood of Christ until a brief mention when He is already twelve years old. There are, however, many apocryphal books that give us a peek at these hidden years. Many of them are fantastical, but there are a few that relate simple but beautiful stories concerning Jesus and His relationship with His father. These hidden years were no doubt filled with the everyday joys and sorrows that families experience all the time. As we have discussed in Chapter 2, Joseph was one who worked in wood and iron to earn a living, however it is also possible that he was a bit of a farmer as well, though not for profit. A rare icon of St. Joseph will depict him standing in front of a tilled field or one which has already yielded its harvest. According to the Infancy Gospel of Thomas, Joseph did in fact have some land suitable for growing food for his family. This account provides a glimpse into the fatherhood of Joseph and the childhood of Christ:

> Now when it was seed time,
> Joseph went forth to sow corn, and Jesus followed after him.
> And when Joseph began to sow, Jesus put forth his hand and took of the corn so much as he could hold in his hand, and scattered it.
> Joseph therefore came at the time of harvest to reap his harvest.
> And Jesus also came and gathered the ears which he had sown, and they made an hundred measures of good corn:
> and he called the poor and the widows and fatherless
> and gave them the corn which he had gained,
> **Infancy Gospel of Thomas 10:1-2**

Once again we are shown that young Jesus, though able to perform miracles, still chooses to work next to His father, in this case harvesting corn. This is a great example of both the humanity and divinity of Jesus Christ being brought out by working with Joseph. Jesus could easily have told the corn to harvest itself; why didn't He? He could have snapped His fingers, and the work would have been finished for His father, but as the old saying goes: "God helps those who help themselves." Instead, He chose to work and go about His days living as a mortal, in the body of a growing child, submitting Himself to the dignity of fatherhood, the head of the family. He submitted Himself to the Law of Moses just like everybody else. Jesus did not come into our world to be our father, but rather our brother.

    How amazed our saint would have been at seeing not only this miracle that Jesus performed as a child, but why He chose to do this. At the end of this account, Jesus and Joseph give the surplus corn to those who are needy, rather than storing it for themselves. There are no show-offs here, no pride, but rather charity and humility. Another account is given to us from the same apocryphal book, this time bringing us to Joseph the Carpenter:

> And Jesus came to be eight years old.
> Now Joseph was a builder and wrought ploughs and yokes for oxen.

> And on a day a certain rich man said unto Joseph:
> Sir, make me a bed serviceable and comely.
> But Joseph was troubled because the beam which he had made ready for the work was short. Jesus said unto him:
> Be not troubled, but take thou hold of this beam
> by the one end and I by the other, and let us draw it out.
>
> And so it came to pass, and forthwith Joseph found it serviceable for that which he desired.
> And he said unto Joseph: Behold, fashion that thou wilt.
> But Joseph when he saw what was done embraced him and said:
> Blessed am I for that God hath given me such a son.
> **Infancy Gospel of Thomas 11:1-2**

Here we see an early example of the compassion that Jesus Christ had for others, especially for His chosen father, Joseph. The two are working side by side, and the boy loves to work with his dad, as most boys that age like to be around their fathers and emulate what they do. No doubt that Joseph could have learned a lot from his Son, but Jesus chooses to respect his intelligence, his hard work, his human nature. Joseph is often depicted in art as being standoffish and out of the picture, but the exact opposite was true. Who would have spent the most time with Christ besides Mother Mary? Joseph, His father. For the first few years of life, the Child would have been reared mostly by His mother while the father went off to work. Once the child grew to suitable age, the father would take over and instruct Him in the ways of life. Joseph would have taught Christ how to read, how to pray, and how to work just like any other father would. This scholastic view of Joseph as teacher is rarely mentioned among the theologians or painted in the arts. However, during the seventeenth century, many artists began to portray him as somewhat of a scholar, with an open book in front of him. In many of these paintings, he is actually pointing to a verse in the book, which we assume is our Holy Scripture, but gazes at the child Jesus. What does this mean to us?

What is Joseph telling us? He was well aware of the prophecies that spoke of a future Messiah, and the depiction of him with the book while looking at Jesus is telling us that Jesus is in fact the Promised One! Let us not assume that just because he worked with his hands, he was illiterate and did not take the time to read the words of the prophets. We are told in Scripture that when Jesus came to this earth, He emptied Himself and did not cling to His divinity, so as to be like one of us. Jesus genuinely willed Himself to learn from His father on earth and to grow as any other Jewish boy would. Joseph was a father, guardian, and teacher to his Son. This "hidden Joseph" of ours is both worker and intellectual, and no doubt he passed these ideals on to Christ our Lord.

> Have this in you which was also in Christ Jesus,
> Who though He was by nature God, did not consider being
> equal to God a thing to be clung to, but emptied Himself ...
> He humbled Himself, becoming obedient ...
> **Philippians 2:5-9**

> My son, conduct your affairs with humility,
> and you will be loved more than a giver of gifts.
> Humble yourself the more ... and you will find favour with God.
> For great is the power of God; by the humble he is glorified.
> **Sirach 3:17-20**

> Hear, O children, a father's instruction,
> be attentive, that you may gain understanding!
> ... When I was my father's child, frail, yet the darling of my mother,
> he taught me, and said to me: "Let your heart hold fast my words!
> Keep my commands, do not forget;
> go not astray from the words of my mouth."
> **Proverbs 4:1-7**

Just how wise Jesus became is shown to us in the Gospel of St. Luke, in which Jesus has already reached adolescence at the age of twelve. This account is known as "The Finding of Jesus in the Temple." Every year, Jewish men were required by the Law to attend three feasts in Jerusalem, which were: Passover, Pentecost, and Tabernacles. Women and children were also allowed to attend these feasts if they wished, but were not required to. In the Gospel, we are told that both Joseph and Mary travelled to Jerusalem for Passover every year, and on this particular occasion Jesus was with them.

> And His parents were wont to go every year to Jerusalem
> At the Feast of the Passover. And when He was twelve years old,
> they went up to Jerusalem according to the custom of the feast.
> **St. Luke 2:41-43**

The relevance of this event in the life of St. Joseph is often overlooked and seen in passing, as Jesus asserts Himself as a wise but respectful boy. Indeed, this mention in the Bible gives us three hidden agendas, which each concern a member of the Holy Family. The first agenda is glorifying the Christ child who demonstrated His deep wisdom and understanding concerning matters of faith and logic. We are told that He sits among the scholars and listens to their words then gives His own opinions and observations. He amazes everyone with His profound insights, and we are told that even the teachers in the temple are astounded by His words!

> ... they found Him in the temple, sitting in the midst of the teachers,
> listening to them and asking them questions.
> And all who were listening to Him
> were amazed at His understanding and His answers.
> **St. Luke 2:46-48**

How did Jesus come to be seated with those in the temple? The Bible tells us that after the Passover celebrations, Joseph and Mary left Jerusalem only to discover that their Son is not part of their caravan! The men and women would usually travel in separate groups, the young children with their mothers. Jesus, however, was already twelve years old, so He would likely have been in Joseph's large group of men. After travelling for one day, Joseph realized that Jesus was not in his group, so he naturally assumed that He was with His mother. After realizing that Jesus was not among their relatives, they journeyed with haste back to Jerusalem. How they must have blamed themselves for losing track of their Son. But a twelve-year-old boy is reaching the age of independence and will often go about on his own. On the third day since leaving Jerusalem they found Him in the temple. Jesus was safe.

> ... it occurred to them to look for Him
> among their relatives and acquaintances.
> And not finding Him, they returned to Jerusalem in search of Him.
> ... they found Him in the temple, sitting in the midst of the teachers,
> ... And when they saw Him, they were astonished.
> **St. Luke 2:44-48**

The second agenda is the role of Mary as mother and a glimpse of her role as intercessor. In this story, her heart is no doubt breaking when she discovers that her Son is missing. Imagine her anxiety and worry searching for her Son, imagine any mother who searches for a missing child. The grief would be almost unbearable. Was her Son lost? Kidnapped? Where was He? Jerusalem would have been a big place for rural people such as Mary and Joseph, and to retrace their steps would be sorrowful and painful. When she and Joseph found their Son, it was Mary who rushed to Jesus and told Him of the anguish they felt when they discovered He was missing. She frantically asked Him why He had done this to them and finds that she cannot help but feel more relief than anything else at finding Him. Since it is she who speaks to Jesus, she is shown as intercessor and speaks on behalf of both Joseph and herself. She takes it upon herself to express the sorrow and affliction felt by both Joseph and herself. No doubt that Joseph felt her pain and relief equally, but allowed her to rush to their Son first.

> And His mother said to Him,
> "Son, why hast thou done so to us? Behold,
> in sorrow thy father and I have been seeking Thee."
> **St. Luke 2:48**

After Our Lady speaks to their Son, the third agenda is given to us, this one concerning Our Blessed Saint Joseph. Jesus' answer to His parents is simple, and many people at first glance think His answer to be one of admonishment or disrespect towards His earthly father Joseph, however the opposite is true.

> And He said to them,
> "How is it you sought me? Did you not know
> that I must be about my Father's business?"
> **St. Luke 2:49**

Some would argue that this response is a direct hit below the belt for Joseph, that Jesus does not recognize the authority of Joseph's fatherhood over Him. Yet, would this not be a breach of the Fourth Commandment given to Moses by God Himself, "Honour thy father and thy mother"? Jesus would not commit this sin. Rather, Jesus was infused with so much knowledge and love of God that He felt so at home in the temple, doing God's work and discussing Him. He was answering in a sincere and direct way. This was by no means a shot at Joseph, after all, isn't God the Father of all mankind? God was the Father of Abraham, David, and Joseph too, though of course not begotten directly by God as Christ was. Joseph would have been so relieved that his Son was alright, and afterwards he would have felt such deep respect and love for his

Son. Though they might not have understood everything concerning their Son, Mary and Joseph no doubt cherished these moments.

What father wouldn't be proud of his son, who managed to capture the hearts and minds of scholars and simpletons alike? Joseph's position of family head is re-established with the closing verses, along with yet another mention of Mary's treasury, which is her maternal heart.

> And He went down with them
> and came to Nazareth, and was subject to them;
> And His mother kept all these things carefully in her heart.
> And Jesus advanced in wisdom and age and grace before God and men.
> **St. Luke 2:51-52**

The Carpenter's Son
Chapter 14: The Servant Departs

> Blessed are the dead who die in the Lord henceforth.
> Yes, says the Spirit, let them rest from their labours,
> for their works follow them.
> **Revelation 13:13**

After the event of the Passover in Jerusalem, we are not given any details about the life of the Holy Family until Christ has already reached the age of thirty-two years. What would have gone on during these years? These years would have been simpler and quieter than the preceding ones, with Joseph and Jesus working side by side at their trade. As mentioned in Chapter 2, an honest day's work brings dignity and the means to support oneself, and father would naturally pass this on to Son. After this period of time, the only mention of Joseph is in reference to where Christ came from and His father's trade, which was passed down to Him, the "carpenter's son."

> "How did this man come by this wisdom and these miracles?
> Is this not the carpenter's son?"
> **St. Matthew 13:54-55**

> … Is not this the carpenter, the son of Mary?"
> **St. Mark 6:3**

It is widely held that St. Joseph had passed away in Nazareth, while Jesus was still at home, before He departed and began His public ministry. Joseph is no longer mentioned, whereas Our Lady is still mentioned during and after this time in Christ's life. The most notable examples are the Wedding Feast of Cana and the Crucifixion of Our Lord, which mention Mary but not her blessed spouse, who surely would have been at her side during these moments.

> … a marriage feast took place at Cana of Galilee,
> And the mother of Jesus was there.
> **St. John 2:1**

> Now there were standing by the cross of Jesus
> His mother and His mother's sister, Mary wife of Cleophas...
> **St. John 19:25**

Surely, if Mary had been invited to the wedding feast, Joseph would have been with her as well, after all, a wedding feast is a gathering of family and friends, but he wasn't. At the crucifixion scene, the mother of Christ stands at the foot of the cross with her sister and with John, the beloved apostle, to whom Jesus entrusts His mother. Had Joseph been alive, there would be no need to place Mary into the care of His best friend. One question that comes to my own mind is, since Jesus had the power to resurrect the dead, such as He did for His friend Lazarus, why didn't He do the same for His father on earth?

This troubled me from time to time, but getting to the heart of the matter has shown me the answer to this. Jesus did not do this for Joseph because it was Joseph's time to go, plain and simple. Joseph had already accomplished the task set out before him by the Most High, which was to raise the Son of God into manhood. Joseph had indeed accomplished what the Lord had asked of him and fulfilled it with the utmost of love, honour, and humility. We do not know what infirmity Joseph succumbed to, but we do know that Jesus would have done everything He could to make this holy man as comfortable as possible during these final moments of earthly life. Joseph is invoked as the Patron of a Happy Death, since we believe that he had the privilege of dying in the arms of Jesus, his Lord and Son, and Mary, his most blessed spouse. According to the Venerable Maria de Agreda, he died in this way:

> Our Lady betook herself to her blessed Son and said to Him:
> "Lord ... I see the hour approaching for the death of Thy servant Joseph.
> I beseech Thee ... let his death be as precious in Thy eyes,
> as the uprightness of his life was pleasing to Thee,
> so that he may depart in peace ...
> Be mindful, my Son, of the humility and love of Thy servant; ... of the fidelity and solicitude by which this just man has supported (us),
> in the sweat of his brow."

> Our Saviour answered: "I will ... assign him a place among the princes of my people, so high that he will be the admiration of the angels and will cause them ... to break forth in highest praise." ... By command of the Lord
> the holy angels ... furnished celestial music,
> mixing their hymns of praise with the benedictions of the sick man.

Then this man of God, turning toward Christ ... in profoundest reverence,
wished to kneel before Him. But the sweetest Jesus, coming near,
received him in His arms, where, reclining his head upon them, Joseph said:
"My highest Lord ... give Thy blessing to Thy servant ...
pardon O most merciful King, (any) faults
which I have committed in Thy service
... I extol and magnify Thee and render eternal and heartfelt thanks to Thee
for having ... chosen me; let Thy greatness and glory be my thanksgiving
for all eternity."

The Redeemer of the world gave him His (blessing), saying:
"My father, rest in peace and in the grace of thy eternal Father and mine;
and to the Prophets and Saints, who await thee in limbo,
bring the joyful news of the approach of their redemption."
At these words of Jesus, and reclining in His arms, the most fortunate
Saint Joseph expired and the Lord himself closed his eyes.
Mystical City of God
Book 5, Chapter 4

In the Gospel of John, Jesus tells us that no one has entered Heaven except for Himself, and that no one will enter it until He has returned there himself. Jesus is the gateway to the Eternal Paradise of Heaven since it was He who conquered the corruption of death, but doesn't the Old Testament tell us that Elias was carried up to Heaven in a chariot of fire?

And it came to pass, when the Lord would take up Elias
into heaven by a whirlwind ... behold a fiery chariot and fiery horses
parted them both asunder: and Elias went up by a whirlwind into heaven.
4 Kings 2:1, 11

This use of the word "heaven" is to mean "into the heavens," which is the sky in general. The prophets of the Old Testament were taken to Limbo, which is a type of waiting room to get into Heaven. Those who have not known Jesus Christ but who have led righteous lives go to this place. This would be the place of the dead, of those who had died before Jesus Himself was crucified and died, only to rise up from His tomb. Earlier, as mentioned in *Mystical City of God*, Joseph is sent to Limbo in order to bring the good news that they would soon see the Messiah and enter into Heaven with Him. The word

"Limbo" refers to the edge of a hem on a garment, so the word is telling us that it is the border of two different places, and that is why this term is used to describe this place of waiting. The Bible itself does not use this word, but the place has been referred to as the Bosom of Abraham. This place was separated by a chasm with the righteous on one side and the wicked on the other. Jesus Himself refers to this place in the Parable of the Unjust Steward:

> "And it came to pass that the poor man died and was borne away
> by the angels into Abraham's bosom;
> but the rich man also died and was buried in hell.
> And lifting up his eyes, being in torments, he saw Abraham afar off
> and Lazarus (the poor man) in his bosom."
> **St. Luke 16:22-24**

St. Augustine of Hippo and St. Hippolytus of Rome both refer to Abraham's Bosom as the place in the afterlife where the spirits await their entry into Heaven, and we cannot doubt that Joseph went to this place of Limbo. His mission on earth had just ended, but an even greater one was about to begin. We picture Joseph in the arms of his beloved Son as he sighs his last breath, with the peace of leaving this world behind to enter into his reward. His years of anxiety, hard work, and dutiful service to his family have paid off and have delivered him into the eternal glory, which we all hope to share. When thinking about this, some of the heartfelt last words of Pope John Paul II come to mind, as he lay on his own deathbed while the immense thousands prayed in St. Peter's square for his peaceful entry into the next life. So too can I picture St. Joseph saying likewise to those who held vigil by his side:

> "I have looked for you.
> Now you have come to me. And I thank you."
> **Pope John Paul II**
> **April 2, 2005**

> "Now Thou dost dismiss Thy servant, O Lord,
> according to Thy word, in peace..."
> **St. Luke 2:29**

The Communion of Saints
Chapter 15: Crown of Eternal Life

"Be thou faithful unto death,
and I will give thee the crown of life."
Revelation 2:10

We are not certain where St. Joseph was buried, but there are a few different suggestions as to where his body lay. Tradition says he was buried in the Valley of Jehoshaphat, located in the foothills of the Mount of Olives. There is a church built there named after Our Lady's Assumption, where it is believed that Mary's body lay before it was taken up to Heaven in the sight of the apostles. This sight also claims to have the tomb of St. Joseph, however it is empty. Whether or not Joseph was assumed body and soul into Heaven, just as his spouse was, is not defined by the Roman Catholic Church. However many saints, such as St. Bernardine of Sienna, St. Francis De Sales, and St. Theresa Avila are in agreement that Jesus did indeed grant Joseph this grace. Since Jesus and Mary ascended into Heaven in the glory of body and soul, so too could we believe this in regards to Joseph.

"How could we doubt that Our Lord
raised glorious St. Joseph up into Heaven, body and soul?
For he had the honour and grace of carrying Him
so often in his blessed arms,
… St. Joseph is therefore in Heaven body and soul, without a doubt."
St. Francis de Sales
Sermon on St. Joseph

… Christ did not deny to Joseph, in heaven,
that intimacy, respect, and high honour which he showed to him
as to a father during his own human life,
but rather completed and perfected it.
St. Bernardine of Sienna
Sermon on St. Joseph, 2

St. Joseph is assuredly in Heaven with his beloved spouse and Our Lord, and he now acts as intercessor for us here on earth. Some people do not believe in praying with the saints and see this as a form of blasphemy, for it pours the entire focus onto the individual rather than onto God. The opposite is true. Many non-Catholics believe that the saints and their statues are worshipped by Catholics, and that we are idolaters, and this has led to much discrimination. There are many books, websites, and videos that create mass confusion and hate towards Catholics, and this is primarily because of misinformation and misinterpretation of Sacred Scripture and Ancient Tradition. To pray means to ask. If you have a friend who is going through some hard times, and they ask you to pray for them, would you refuse them? I would hope not. This is an act of friendship and of hope. We can use all the prayers we can get in this world we live in, and the more the better.

Some people believe that when we die, we are immobile and can no longer pray. What do these people think we are to do in Heaven? Just float around and be happy every day? No, there is more to that. St. Therese of Lisieux, for example, planned to work hard in Heaven for those she left behind. Shortly before her death, she left us with these words:

> "After my death I will let fall a shower of roses…
> I will spend my Heaven doing good on earth."
> **St. Therese of Lisieux**

When in Heaven, would we not want to keep helping our family and friends on earth with the help of our prayers for them? Just because we are no longer living on earth, it doesn't mean that God stops listening to us. Is God not in Heaven? Wouldn't we be closer to God, more than ever? Why would the Heavenly Father stop hearing our pleas? He wouldn't. St. Joseph, the man closest to Christ, would undoubtedly pray for those who ask for his help. Just as Jesus listened to him on earth, so too does He listen to St. Joseph in Heaven. Joseph is not over Jesus in any way, but rather the humble servant of the Lord, but Jesus chooses to honour the requests of the man who raised him from infancy into manhood. He still honours His parents in Heaven.

Above all, we worship God, but isn't it nice to have extra help by getting those who found favour with God to pray for us as well? God is glorified in St. Joseph because God gave him the graces needed to live his life and enter into paradise. God has given us a prime example of what it is to serve the Lord with all your heart and mind, and this exemplar of true devotedness to the Supreme Lord is humble St. Joseph. God wants us to pray for each other so that all will be saved and come to a greater understanding of who He is. Does asking someone to pray for you interfere in your relationship with God? No, it enhances it.

> And another angel came and stood before the altar,
> having a golden censer; and there was given to him much incense,
> that he might offer it with the prayers of all the saints
> upon the golden altar which is before the throne.
> And with the prayers of the saints there went up before God,
> from the angel's hand, the smoke of the incense.
> **Revelation 8:3-5**

Joseph is now in Heaven and aids us by his prayers and protection. If ever a man existed who deserves the splendour of Heaven it is St. Joseph, the just man who lived an honourable and holy life. He made plenty of sacrifices and offered them up to the Lord in supplication for those who do not believe in the Lord. He is united with his beloved spouse Mary and with Jesus the Eternal Son, whom he raised as his own flesh and blood. His trials reminiscent of the exile into Egypt have long faded, his anxieties have been calmed, and his rough hands, which supported his family, have been soothed by the Divine Healer, who crowns his achievements and tribulations with everlasting life.

> … when he has been tried, he will receive the crown of life
> which God has promised to those who love Him.
> **St. James 1:12**

The Communion of Saints
Chapter 16: In God's Own Time

> ... one day with the Lord is as a thousand years,
> and a thousand years is as one day.
> **2 St. Peter 8**

For centuries, St. Joseph has remained hidden from us in the background of the big picture, only emerging when he was needed. But everything is done in God's time and ultimately His Divine Will is accomplished exactly when He sees fit. The first millennium was reserved for the sole exploration of who Jesus Christ was and continues to be for us. It was a time for discernment and meditation on the Word of God, Who came to save us from our sins so that we may find eternal joy in the comforts of Heaven. We were given insights into the life, death, and resurrection of Our Lord in order to understand God's plan for mankind. Jesus is the New Adam who came to fulfill what was written in the books of the Prophets and to lead us in the direction of continuation. He left us the gift of the Holy Spirit in order for us to continue His work on earth, in order to sustain the Mystical Body of Christ, which He left behind for us. This Mystical Body is the Church, and the perfect blueprint for this was left for us as well. Mother Mary is this blueprint. She is the new Eve.

> For just as by the disobedience of the one man
> the many were constituted sinners,
> so also by the obedience of the One (Jesus)
> the many will be constituted just.
> **Romans 5:19**

The next millennium would be focussed on knowing Christ more intimately through those closest to Him. Who better to show us how to love Jesus than his own mother? If she is not a part of God's plan, then why did she not die early on, just as Joseph had? Because she still had a purpose on this earth. That is why she was entrusted to mankind at the foot of the cross. These years were open to teach us how to emulate her and lead by her example of humility, in true love for Christ. She is not in the way of Christ—she leads us straight to Him! She guides us to her dearly beloved Son who is never too proud to accept us, even from His mother's hands. Jesus is the only mediator between God the Father and us, since Jesus was the only one begotten of the Father as both God and man. Mary is there to draw us in closer in union with her Son and is one of His great disciples. In the Gospel of St. Luke, someone from the crowd praises Mary for giving birth to Jesus, but Jesus says instead that she is blessed because she has heard the Word of God and held true to it. She lived her faith strongly, rather than relying on one single moment to be the cause of her blessedness. She is blessed for many reasons, the most important being that she lived for God and kept true to her faith in Him.

> "Blessed is the womb that bore Thee, and the breasts that nursed Thee."
> But (Jesus said) "Rather, blessed are they who hear
> the Word of God and keep it."
> **St. Luke 11:27-28**

The third millennium seems to be open to Joseph, the Guardian of the Redeemer, who up till recently was hidden from us. We are discovering his role not only within the pious walls of the church, but also within the story of salvation! We are learning about his role as Head of the Holy Family. Why is this important? Why do we need Joseph? Why should we honour him? Because Jesus does. Joseph has remained hidden from us up till now because now more than ever we need a human father to teach us how to live. We need a human father to show us what life really is and how to respect it. It is in this millennium that the ethics in life are under attack more than ever. Abortion is rampant and is seen as an acceptable alternative to taking responsibility for one's actions in creating a life. If by Divine Providence God hadn't willed the safety of Jesus, by the person of Joseph, then Jesus would have died as a baby. Now, we see that children are being murdered not only right after they are brought into this world, but even before! Who protected the unborn child within Mary's womb? Joseph, by the grace of God. Who made sacrifices for his family and put their needs above his own? Joseph. Who took responsibility for loving and supporting his family—even in the hardest of times? Joseph. Now more than ever, in this world in which we live, we need a man to show us how to live a just life.

> "O God, behold [your] shield,
> and look upon the face of your anointed ...

> I had rather lie at the threshold of the house of my God
> than to dwell in the tents of the wicked ...
> O Lord of Hosts, happy the [man] who trust[s] in You!"
> **Psalm 84:9-12**

God and His followers have never been under attack more than right now. We need Joseph's prayers for a world gone wrong, and we need him as our example to follow Jesus to the Father and to live His Divine Will. The Bible tells us that for a time things would remain hidden from us, because the time was not yet right to discover these hidden things. Well, now is surely the time for all to be revealed. We see it, and we have to accept it rather than bury it under so called "rationality" and science. Certain things were hidden from us because we were not yet ready for them, but one cannot suppress the Will of God, and these hidden things have started to surface for us to know and meditate upon them.

> And I, brethren, could not speak to you as to spiritual men ...
> you were not yet ready for it ...
> **1 Corinthians 3:1-2**

> For there is nothing hidden that will not be made manifest,
> nor anything concealed that will not be known and come to light.
> **St. Luke 8:17**

The Communion of Saints
Chapter 17: Final Thoughts

"To be a father means above all to be at the service of life and growth. Saint Joseph, in this sense, gave proof of great devotion. For the sake of Christ he experienced persecution, exile, and the poverty that this entails. He had to settle far from his native town. His only reward was to be with Christ. His readiness to do all these things illustrates the words of Saint Paul: "It is Christ the Lord whom you serve" (Col 3:24).
Pope Benedict XVI
Yaoundé, Cameroon, March 18, 2009

It is hard to believe that I have already gotten to this ending point of our book. I feel as though I have only grazed the surface of what could be said about Blessed St. Joseph of Nazareth, and yet when I try to get it down on paper, my mind seems to want to express too many thoughts at once, and therefore only a particle of what can be said is, in fact, said. For me, this has been a valuable experience because in the process of writing this little book, I have come to a greater appreciation of not only St. Joseph, but the entire Holy Family.

Researching St. Joseph has led me to many places and one of these places is the Holy Bible. To be honest I had never really read the Bible, but it was in doing this project that I came to discover it, full its of history, parables, poetry, songs, miracles, and wisdom! The Bible is so rich and exhaustive that to sit down and read it cover to cover does not seem possible. My priest, Father Paul, suggested to me that it is often rewarding to just open the Bible to some random page, point, and start reading. It's funny how sometimes when you do this you seem to point to exactly what you need to read. There's always something for us. It was in searching for certain passages to use for this book that I would come across something else I could use later on, and from that I would find something I could have used earlier. So the entire process was a sort of game of tag. "Chapter 13, you're it!" TAG!, "Chapter 3, now *you're* it!" Back and forth, back and forth, but ultimately it had to lead to this closing chapter of my final thoughts.

St. Joseph, in union with the Blessed Virgin Mary, has brought me into a closer union with the Eternal Son, Jesus Christ, and writing this little book has helped me to get there. I look back on the rough handwritten notes I made and am awestruck that they have become what they are now. I am not a theologian or a professional writer, as you can probably tell by my style of writing, but I believe that sometimes we can go over the top with the education we have. We get so caught up in the titles we have earned that when we write, we become inaccessible and out of reach for those who are very much down to earth. I'm not sure how to close this, so perhaps the Pontiffs can help us with that, by adding a few words of their own, on our Beloved Saint.

Fathers of families find in Joseph
the best personification of paternal solicitude and vigilance;
Spouses, a perfect example of love, of peace, and of conjugal fidelity;
Virgins at the same time find in him the model
and protector of virginal integrity.
Pope Leo XIII
Quamquam Pluries, August 15, 1889

All the saints in glory assuredly merit honour and particular respect,
but it is evident that Saint Joseph possesses a just title to a more sweet,
more intimate and penetrating place in our hearts, belonging to him alone...
Here we are able to estimate completely all the greatness of Saint Joseph,
not only by reason of the fact that he was close to Jesus and Mary,
but also by the shining example he has given of all virtues...
Pope John XXIII
Allocution on March 19, 1959

This just man, who bore within himself
the entire heritage of the Old Covenant,
was also brought into the "beginning" of the
New and Eternal Covenant in Jesus Christ.
May he show us the paths of this saving Covenant as we
stand at the threshold
of the next millennium, in which there must be a continuation and further
development of the "fullness of time" that belongs the
ineffable mystery of the Incarnation of the Word.
Pope John Paul II
Redemptoris Custos, August 15, 1989

The life of Saint Joseph, lived in obedience to God's word, is an eloquent sign for all the disciples of Jesus who seek the unity of the Church. His example helps us to understand that it is only by complete submission to the will of God that we become effective workers in the service of his plan to gather together all mankind into one family, one assembly, one 'ecclesia.'
Pope Benedict XVI
Yaoundé, Cameroon, March 18, 2009

And so with the end of these Papal musings, so comes the end to this little book. May we never neglect to meditate upon the life of the "just man," predestined above all others to be the chosen father of God, nor of his immaculate spouse, Mary most pure. It is upon meditating on these things that we become fully aware of the life of Jesus Christ and the humanity He took on in order to become like one of us. Now we must strive to become like Him, and who better to help us with this than His parents, who know Him more intimately than anyone else? May Blessed Saint Joseph draw us closer into the mystery of Our Beloved Jesus and may he intercede for us, in our spiritual and temporal needs, before the glorious throne of God. Amen.

March 25, 2009

The Communion of Saints
Chapter 18: Be Prayerful

The Gloria
Glory be to the Father, and to the Son, and to the Holy Spirit,
as it was in the beginning, is now and ever shall be,
world without end.
Amen.

Hail Joseph
Hail Joseph, Son of David, God is with you!
Blessed are you amongst men,
and blessed is Our Lord Jesus Christ!
Holy Joseph, Guardian of the Redeemer
and of His holy Virgin Mother,
Pray for us and be with us,
now and as we sigh our last breath.
Amen.

Ancient Prayer to Joseph (circa A.D. 50)[7]
O St. Joseph whose protection is so great,
so strong, so prompt before the Throne of God,
I place in you all my interests and desires.
O St. Joseph assist me by your powerful intercession
and obtain for me from your Divine Son
all spiritual blessings through Jesus Christ, Our Lord; so that having engaged
here below your Heavenly power I may offer my Thanksgiving and
Homage to the most Loving of Fathers.
O St. Joseph, I never weary contemplating you with Jesus asleep in your arms.
I dare not approach while He reposes near your heart.
Press Him in my name and kiss His fine Head for me,
and ask Him to return the Kiss when I draw my dying breath.
St. Joseph, Patron of departing souls, pray for us.
Amen.

Prayer to Live the Divine Will

Good St. Joseph, I salute you as the Virgin Father chosen by God,
to be the loving guardian of Jesus and spouse of Our Lady!
Pray for us who call on you, and by your leading example,
help us to live the Divine Will, in obedience and compassion,
for the greater glory of the Eternal Son.
Amen.

The Communion of Saints
Chapter 19: The Feast of St. Joseph

Solemnity of Saint Joseph (St. Joseph's Day)
March 19:
First inserted into the General Roman Calendar for celebration in 1621 by Pope Gregory XV, though this date had already been informally dedicated to St. Joseph as early as the tenth century.

This date also fittingly serves as "Fathers' Day" in some Catholic countries such as Portugal, Spain, and Italy.

St. Joseph the Patron of the Universal Church
Third Wednesday after Easter:
Between 1870 and 1955, this feast day celebrated the title given to St. Joseph by Pope Pius IX. This feast was removed in 1955 by Pope Pius XII.

St. Joseph the Worker
May 1:
Instituted in 1955 by Pope Pius XII, to counter the Communist holiday of "May Day."

St. Joseph the Betrothed (celebrated by the Eastern Churches)
First Sunday after Christmas:
St. Joseph is commemorated on the Sunday after the Nativity. If there is no Sunday between December 25 and January 1, his feast day, along with King David and St. James the Greater, is moved to December 26.

Feast of the Holy Family
First Sunday after Christmas:
Instituted by Pope Leo XIII. Should there be no Sunday between Christmas and New Year's Day, the feast is moved to December 30.

Espousals of Mary and Joseph
January 23:

Approved in 1546 by Pope Paul III to celebrate the holy union of Mary and Joseph.

Bibliography

The Holy Bible. St. Joseph New Catholic Edition. Catholic Book Publishing Company, 1962.

D'Agreda, Ven. Maria. *The Mystical City of God*. Tan Publishing Company, 2006.

Dods, Marcus, and George Reith. *Ante-Nicene Fathers, vol. 1,* Christian Literature Publishing Company, 1885.

James, M. R. *The New Testament Apocrypha*. Apocryphile Press, 2004.

Pope Leo XIII. *Quamquam Pluries*. Libreria Editrice Vaticana. *http://www.vatican.va/holy_father/leo_xiii/encyclicals/documents/hf_l-xiii_enc_15081889_quamquam-pluries_en.html*

Pope John Paul II. *Redemptoris Custos*. Libreria Editrice Vaticana, *http://www.vatican.va/holy_father/john_paul_ii/apost_exhortations/documents/hf_jp-ii_exh_15081989_redemptoris-custos_en.html*

Pope Benedict XVI. *St. Joseph Lived His Fatherhood Fully*. Speech at Yaoundé, Cameroon, 2009, *http://www.zenit.org/article-25407?l=english*

Made in the USA
Lexington, KY
10 January 2010